E.J. (Ted) Hart

Ain't it Hell

Bill Peyto's "Mountain Journal"

Summerthought

Banff, Alberta

AIN'T IT HELL: BILL PEYTO'S "MOUNTAIN JOURNAL"

Published by

Summerthought

Summerthought Publishing
PO Box 2309
Banff, AB T1L 1C1
Canada
www.summerthought.com

Printing History
1st edition —1995
2nd edition—2008

Library and Archives Canada Cataloguing in Publication

Hart, E. J. (Edward John), 1946-
Ain't it Hell: Bill Peyto's "Mountain Journal" / E.J. Hart.—2nd ed.

ISBN 978-0-9782375-5-4

1. Peyto, Bill, 1869-1943—Fiction. I. Title.

PS8565.A6647A38 2008   C813.54   C2008-900045-5

Front cover photo: Bill Peyto. © Whyte Museum of the Canadian Rockies (NA66 577)
Printed in Canada by Friesens

For the Spirit of Bill Peyto,
which still roams the backcountry
of Banff National Park

FOREWORD

Who is Bill Peyto?

Bill Peyto is a person the visitor to Banff cannot avoid.

One first meets Bill staring steely-eyed from the sign welcoming visitors and providing directional information at the entrance to the town of Banff. As they make their way down Banff Avenue past Caribou Street, their eyes are drawn to the second storey of a handsome building where the same rough-hewn mountain man adorns the logo advertising "Wild Bill's Restaurant and Saloon." A right turn down Caribou and a left on Bear leads them past "Peyto Place," named after Bill and his brothers. Here a picture of Bill in his bowler hat and tie, which won an award at the Toronto Fair in 1913, dominates a display window.

If the visitor should continue on to Lake Louise and stop for lunch at the Lake Louise Alpine Centre, the familiar face and the name "Bill Peyto's Cafe" will greet them. Onwards from Lake Louise up the Icefields Parkway will lead to one of the most stunning viewpoints in the Canadian Rockies – the snout of the massive Peyto Glacier emptying its meltwaters into the aquamarine waters of Peyto Lake at the foot of Peyto Peak.

Who is Bill Peyto?

Bill Peyto is Banff's most legendary figure.

Stories of Bill's amazing feats in the days before the turn-of-
the-century when he guided the first alpinists to scale the
Rockies' highest peaks are well known. Tales of his bringing
a lynx into a bar, shooting a grizzly bear with a pistol, or res-
cuing a stranded woman climber from a precarious ledge
are still told in Banff watering holes today much as they
were fifty years ago. His accomplishments as one of the ear-
liest national park wardens patrolling the trails of his district with the stealth of a mountain lion are the foundation
for the *esprit de corps* of the modern-day warden service.

Who is Bill Peyto?

Bill Peyto is an enigma.

Except for his warden diaries, which have long since disappeared, Bill Peyto did not record the many and varied facets
of a long and fascinating life. His early activities as a guide
and outfitter are related in the books of some of the alpinists
he accompanied, such as Wilcox, Collie and Outram; peri-
odic newspaper articles relating to his exploits and personal life sprinkle the pages of the Banff *Crag and Canyon*; and
some stories lived clearly in the minds of Banff old-timers
who spoke of him in interviews or wrote of him in memoirs.

Despite his obvious importance in the history of the Canadian Rockies, no-one has previously documented his life. I have written the stories of many of Bill's compatriots of the trail — Tom Wilson, Jimmy Simpson, the Brewster brothers — but I could never find ample material to accomplish his biography.

But some painstaking research has turned up many signposts in Bill's life — not enough for that biography, but plenty for a work of historical fiction using the known facts as a basis around which to structure the story. *Ain't It Hell* is Bill's story, as closely as I can recreate it over fifty years after his death.

Who is Bill Peyto?

Read on and you shall discover who Bill Peyto is.

Prologue

Ebenezer William Peyto was born at Welling, Kent on February 14, 1869, the third son in a family of nine. His father Augustus was a farm bailiff and his mother Ellen a servant. The family name had originally been spelled PETO, but his great-grandfather, a military tailor in Woolwich, had a nameplate made that had been misspelled PEYTO (pronounced pea toe*) and the error stuck.*

At the time of Bill's youth Welling was a farming area about nine miles from London (now part of Greater London), and so his upbringing was mainly rural. His parents were hardworking, godfearing folk and Bill learned at an early age that to succeed one had to depend on himself and not be afraid of work. His father was active in the Congregationalist Church, so religion played a large part in the family's life. Like his brothers and sisters, Bill attended an ordinary public school, Foster's Endowed Church of England School, where he learned the basics of the 3Rs.

It is possible that as a teenager Bill spent some time in the British Army, but if so he quickly left and set out for America, like so many other youth of his time who could see no future in England. He arrived at Halifax in late February, 1887, just after his eighteenth birthday. From there he headed west on the newly completed CPR line and within a month of his landing was working for the railway company clearing a snowslide in the Kicking Horse Pass. He stayed in this area for some time, living at Moberly, near Golden, B.C., during 1887 and probably 1888, alternately working for the CPR and prospecting. His knowledge of geology and paleontology seems to have been developed very early on, and despite his lack of formal education he was an avid reader and collector of books on these topics and quickly became self-taught.

Bill next turns up near Cochrane about 1890. He settled on a piece of land in the Montreal Valley west of Cochrane not far from the Ghost River. This area was being taken up by small ranchers at the time and that was likely Bill's intention as well, although he did not actually file a homestead claim until several years later. He appears to have spent little time there, being much more attracted to the mountains, and probably began living at least part of the time in Banff about the same year. In this period he began his prospecting activities in the area: Walter Wilcox recorded in The Rockies of Canada *that while exploring Prospector's Valley in 1899 he came across the remains of Peyto's old mining camp that he had abandoned some years before when deserted by his horses. He would also have begun trapping in the winter at this point, and in the summer is thought to have spent some time working for Superintendent George Stewart of Rocky Mountains Park building trails and doing other early park development work.*

Bill's varied lifestyle, his activities in the backcountry and his keen powers of observation would have quickly made him knowledgeable of the mountains. It was not surprising, therefore, that Tom Wilson, who had begun his outfitting and guiding service in Banff in 1893, would turn to Bill as a packer and guide. Tom had first met Bill at Moberly in 1887 and he had a homestead at Morleyville, not far from Bill's, so the two were well acquainted.

Here we pick up the story in Bill's "mountain journal" . . .*

*Although Bill had a good command of the English language, his written grammar and punctuation left something to be desired. I have chosen to use language consistent with his vocabulary but correct grammar and punctuation in creating his journal to make an easier read.

I
1895

June 1

I recently received a letter from my dear old mother back in Welling telling me how much she misses me and giving me the dickens for not writing more often. With this roving life I lead and her religious outlook, I'm not sure how much of the tale she'd really like to hear. But, being a good son, I did write back and tell her I'll try to mend my ways and write more often. I know it's a bit queer but I've decided to start keeping this journal as a way of recording what she might find interesting, and, God willing, some day I'll give it to her. I won't be a slave to it and I'm not sure how long I'll stick with it, but I'll try put something down when it's worthwhile and the spirit moves me.

II
1895

June 15

Rode up from the ranch yesterday on Chiniquay, my best mount, who's sporting his new brand. I thought it was about time to register a mark if I'm going to keep a few head on the grass there. I decided on the form of a fossilized brachiopod, looking like this ⊚ , as I wanted something that would be special and reflected my interests.

Today I went over to see Tom Wilson. I'll be damned if he isn't going to keep that pack outfit he got together a few summers ago around for another kick at the cat. I know he did a bit of horse packing for some of those railway types and government surveyors and he has taken the odd dude from the east out hunting and exploring, but I wasn't convinced he could make a go of it and keep bread on the table for that growing brood of his.

I can recall in '87 when he blew into Moberly with those two bedraggled Englishmen in tow after chopping his way down the Blaeberry. I thought this guiding thing was a bit strange at the time, but I've got to admit with the number of easterners with a far away look in their eyes getting off the Pacific Express down at the station these days he may be on to something.

Tom knows that I understand these mountains nearly as well as he, and I can sure handle those hairbrained cayuses better than anybody in these parts, so he asked me to come on board. This government business is sure wearing thin and I'm yearning to see some fresh country, so I just may give it a shake.

June 18
Tom spoke with me again today. He says that he's got that Barrett fellow from Chicago who he took out to Assiniboine in '93 coming back for another try at her scalp along with another one of those stateside business types. He asked me to go along and help Ralph Edwards, who he wants to put in charge. Ralph's an all-right sort — he hails from Ramsgate, not far from my dearly departed Welling. But he's younger than me, doesn't know the ways of the mountains and the wild things as well as I do, and has been working the mines at Canmore for quite awhile breathing coal dust instead of clear mountain air. But it's Tom's outfit, and I guess if I'm going to work for him I'll have to prove myself.

We're supposed to leave about the beginning of July, but this damn weather's been so backward we'd have to fit those ponies with snowshoes to make it through some of that high country. I get the feeling I'm going to earn that four bits a day Tom's promised!

June 25
I'm just back from a scout around to eyeball the trail we're going to follow. Tom explained the route he took with Barrett two years ago by way of the Simpson Pass and River, and since I hadn't been over there before I thought I should see it myself. It's mostly an old Indian trail — one of the old timers at Morley told me they refer to it as Shuswap Pass, so it must have been used by that tribe many years ago.

Just as I expected there's lots of snow on top and its going to be hard lines to get through. But I can see it's special country — nice open meadows with interesting quartz outcroppings in the limestone that I couldn't really get a good look at because of the drifts. I'm going to have to spend a bit of time there once things clear off a bit doing a little prospecting.

July 1
Well, they're celebrating this Dominion's birth today —its 28th — and its worth celebrating too. Canada is everything that dear old England isn't — freedom to roam in these beautiful hills seeing no one but the wild things, freedom to say what's on a bloke's mind without looking over his shoulder, and freedom to earn a grubstake by using brains and wits instead of depending on one's station of birth.

Speaking of earning a living, we're now deep into preparing for this excursion to Assiniboine and I'm spending most of my time down at Tom's corral on Buffalo Street sorting out supplies and getting those cayuses tamed down for their first work of the season. Some of those knotheads are going to take a bit of work before we get them straightened out, but I can tell Chiniquay can't wait to get back into that high country.

Our party has grown as Mr. Barrett and his friend Mr. Porter have agreed to combine forces with Walter Wilcox. Tom knows Wilcox because he provided he and Samuel Allen with supplies two years ago when they were exploring the Lake Louise area. Wilcox had just graduated from Yale then and now goes to Columbia University, so he must have some sense. He's been hanging around Tom's too, fidgeting and waiting for this weather to break. I can't ever remember seeing anyone so neatly turned out — he's always dressed like he just stepped out of a gent's shop. I'll have to watch and see if he's really got the mustard when we start heading into that heavy timber the other side of Simpson Pass.

July 5
We're finally getting off tomorrow, even though the weather is still ornery. I'll wear that buckskin shirt I had the Indian woman make me last year and two pairs of pants, as I'm sure my legs are going to take a beating in some of the heavy going. I'll carry my cartridge belt, Colt and best hunting knife around my middle. Even though they'll make things a mite awkward, I can't be too careful with some of those bears and polecats I know are out there.

Tom has decided to send two other men along with Ralph and myself to help cook and care for the nine horses. One is a bloke by the name of Harry Lang, who tells me his father owns a hotel at Brighton and insisted he come to Canada to make his way. A lot of my countrymen get a regular stipend from home to make sure they don't darken the family doors again, but I sure don't need to be bribed to enjoy this country. Anyway, he seems like a kindly sort and I'm sure we'll get by as long as he holds up his end of the bargain. These Yanks sure are going to get an earful around the campfire at night with all us Mother England types swapping yarns.

July 6
There was a bit of kicking and biting as we headed off today and a few of the packs got a bit shook up while these ponies

got figured out who's going to be at the head of the line. Wilcox has this big camera outfit and says he's going to take photographs and write a story — I don't know about that but I do know his stuff is not the easiest to keep on a pack-saddle. We went ahead with the packtrain up Healy Creek about five miles and the dudes walked into camp later in the afternoon. They called us from across the creek and I had to use Chiniquay to ferry them over. They were a wet and unhappy lot but we soon had them fed and comfortable on the bough beds we had made in their tents with their clothes drying in front of the fire.

July 11
The last five days have been some fun as just about every-thing that could go wrong has. I somehow think that may be the nature of this game.

I guess I've made my graduation to guide. After leaving our first camp we marched for six hours up the north fork and camped within easy reach of Simpson Pass. When we put up that night Ralph found he had lost his axe and decided to go back for it so he wouldn't have to play beaver on the downed timber that awaited us. We thought he would be back in a few hours, but I haven't seen his hide since and have had to take over the outfit.

After a day floundering through the snow up on the divide, we went over onto the Pacific side and it warmed up con-siderably. We were soon in banks of wildflowers and our spirits were bubbling like hot springs until we hit that heavy timber near the Simpson River. The next day one of the pack horses got lamed up in a rough spot and while we were taking a short cut through a mossy place I had discovered during my reconnaisance trip the poor beast broke his leg. There was nothing for it but to plug him where he lay and repack the duffel on Chiniquay. I hoped to find a campspot close by but we soon entered a high valley full of rockslides and it was only after nine hours on the move that we finally put down roots in a delightful spot about 2000 feet above the river.

Today we continued upward and again hit snow — in some places it was six feet deep and we had to go ahead and beat down a path so the horses could get through. Then, after ascending a high ridge, we were met with a view of a desolate valley of fire-killed timber, but we were so bushed that we couldn't go on. Tonight we are camped on the edge of a ravine with a swamp full of birds behind it. The dudes seem to like it, but it don't quite strike me as ideal. One consolation — we can finally see the top of Mt. Assiniboine, even though it is only faintly through the smoke from all the damn forest fires.

July 21
Old Chiniquay and me have sure been on the go some.

The day after my last writing we reached the base of Assiniboine and camped by a beautiful lake that nestles up to it. I've seen pictures of the Matterhorn, and I have to agree with the dudes, who think this bears a striking resemblance.

Ralph had not caught up to us and I was worried he had drowned fording the creek or been eaten by a grizzly attracted by the food we had left for him. After getting the camp set up as a base for the gentlemen's explorations, I mounted Chiniquay and headed back for Banff on the double quick. I rode hard for three days and could see that someone had used a few of our camps, but Ralph was nowhere to be found. When I reached town I reported into Tom, who told me Ralph had followed our trail for four days but then had lost it and returned to Banff. I opined that he possessed very little Indian in him if he couldn't follow the trail of six horses headed to a peak as big as Assiniboine, but Tom was inclined to send him back out. He gave us a spare cayuse to take the place of the lost one, and after we rousted out Ralph and got him reloaded we hightailed it back here.

July 29
I've got to admit, I've had to change my opinion about Wilcox and Barrett — these are two tough dudes. We've just completed a two day tramp around Assiniboine that would make a mountain goat tired.

After returning from Banff, W. & B. were itching for some work and on the 26th we set out on foot to see the south side. I'm not partial to log work, but it would have helped here, because after scrambling up and down valley walls of some 2000 feet we encountered a burned over area where we crawled over blowdown timber for hours on end. Late in the afternoon we had to stop from sheer exhaustion, and Wilcox said he thought we looked black as coal heavers from the charcoaled tree trunks. I quickly made us three lean-tos by propping up our blankets on a rocky ledge and cooked up a feed of fat bacon, hardtack and tea. Then I used a little trick to make us a mattress, gathering up some dried moss and spreading it on the rocks, and it allowed us to spend a passably comfortable night.

The next day we started off early skirting the peak's spurs, and by late morning we had come to a high ridge blocking our way to the north fork of the Cross River. We began ascending it but once we topped out there was a huge vertical wall of rock about 500 feet high facing us, and Porter and I sat down to contemplate with a pipe while Wilcox went off to take some photographs of the south side. While resting I studied the rock face and noted that some sort of game trail seemed to traverse it. When Wilcox returned I tried to explain it, but they couldn't quite get it, so having opened my mouth I now had to demonstrate my point and make like a goat. It wasn't too bad, so while the gents watched I scrambled up and found a steep snow slope near the top, which I didn't much like but took on just the same. It worked and I soon had W. & B. following me to the top of what proved to be a 9,000 foot ridge and the key to reaching the north fork valley.

We raced down the scree on the other side, passing into a veritable garden of trees, grass and wildflowers near the river. We discovered a trail and while following it met another party of Tom's composed of Messrs. Allen and Smith, who were out exploring for a month. After a brief confab we were on our way again, travelling in the valley for about six miles before swinging north around Assiniboine's east side. I had hoped to reach base camp that day, but we again ran into the infernal burnt stuff and stumbled around in the dark until I had to make a rough bivouac and feed my dudes before they collapsed. Rising before day-

light, we were on our way again at 4 and into camp for a real
breakfast by 6:30. I didn't let on, but I was dog tired after
tramping fifty-one miles in less than two days and can
imagine how they felt having come so recently from their
office desks.

August 6
Well this blasted trip is finally over and we're back in Banff
safe and sound.

The dudes wanted to do some more exploring after our trip
around Assiniboine, so I suggested we take the Simpson to
the Vermilion River and then follow it over on to the Bow. It
took two days to reach the Vermilion and going up it proved
pretty tricky as we had to constantly cross and recross to
find a route for the horses. At one bad spot a pack horse got
swept downstream but luckily got caught in an eddy and
tried to climb up on a bar. I could see he wouldn't make it,
so calling to Ralph I jumped in and we managed, by pulling
on various parts of the cayuse's anatomy, to get him up and
save his infernal hide. Meanwhile, the dudes were left
stranded surrounded by deep rapids and after I got back up
on Chiniquay I had to go over and ferry them to shore. It
was rough going for the old fellow but he showed his pluck.
Wilcox held on around my middle so tight I could barely
breathe, but even at that there were a few moments when I
thought he would be washed off.

Near the pass we followed a stream coming in from the west
to explore a remarkable canyon we had heard of, and it was
sure worth the detour. The rock here is almost entirely
quartzite, appearing much like marble, and the water flows

through high narrow walls before plunging into a huge hole with a roar like a locomotive. These mountains never cease to amaze me with a new experience at every turn.

We forded the Bow on the fourth with the bulldog-flies driving the horses near crazy. Wouldn't you know after traipsing through all that rough country with Wilcox's precious camera and plates intact the packhorse would decide to give them a bath just when we about had it licked. He seemed a might upset, so when we got to Castle I got one of the section men to flag down a freight to take them directly into Banff and his humour improved somewhat. We'll have to see if he blames it on me when he's talking to Tom.

On our way back into Banff, Ralph and I stopped for a little visit with Dave White and his sister Lizzie at the railway siding where he's the section foreman. We had a nice dinner and some entertainment from their violins, making a very pleasant conclusion to a rough few days.

III
1895

August 10

The Gods must be smiling as Wilcox isn't too provoked after all. No sooner did I get to Banff than Tom told me my services had been found to be of a high order and I had been requested for a further expedition. It seems Wilcox wants to have a peek at the Waputehk Range north of Laggan where he has heard that the rocks, glaciers and lakes are of much interest. Having spent some time in that country myself I can certainly agree. I'm to take a man with me in a few days to start chopping out the downed timber on the old tote road so we can save a little time.

August 13

Arthur Arnold and yours truly dragged our hinders into Laggan this evening after two of the most miserable days of trail clearing it has been my misfortune to endure. That Godforsaken tote road the CPR pushed a few miles up the Bow back in '83 may have seemed like the road to the Promised Land then, but its more like the way to Hades now. The forest fires have done their devilish work and the burnt timber is piled up like the remains of some gigantic bonfire in Hell. Combined with a heatwave and a fresh hatch of bulldogs and mosquitoes every day, it made for some blue air while we toiled at it.

There was one consolation — while we were working we camped at the cabin of that old prospector Hunter, who has been roaming those parts for a few years. We shared an evening pipe and compared notes on the rocks and the possibility of claims in the area. He's originally from the States and showed me a few of the geology books he brought with him, but from a quick glance I don't think his material stands a candle to mine. It's hard to beat Lyell's Manual of Elementary Geology and his Principles of Geology along with Dana's two books. I got the idea he was onto something around Baker Creek, but as soon as I expressed an interest he clammed up tighter than a bar on Sunday. Can't say as I blame him — if it was him asking me I'd tell him to mind his own Goddamned business too!

August 15
We pulled out from Laggan about noon yesterday with two packhorses and three saddle horses for Wilcox, myself and Arthur, who is going to cook. But the trip almost ended before it began because of a little set-to we had with a freight train.

Just as we left town we were getting the cayuses sorted out as we travelled along beside the track. We were crossing near a curve, which in hindsight was none too smart of me, when a locomotive came steaming around the bend. I looked up to see Arthur and Wilcox paralyzed with fear and knew I couldn't expect any help from that quarter. As quick as lightning, I slapped the nearest packhorse over the head with the end of my reins while grabbing the halter rope of the other. I spurred Chiniquay hard and he didn't let me down, leaping sideways like he'd been bit by a rattlesnake. The packhorse followed just as that black engine of death roared by, rippling the hair on his tail. I happened to glance up and was staring into the astonished eyes of the engineer as his face flashed by, looking like he'd just seen a ghost.

As we carried on, Wilcox commented favourably on our trail clearing and I told him it was a good thing he hadn't been around for it or his ears would have turned permanently red. He started talking about the history of forest fires in the mountains in the writings of the explorers and fur traders, mentioning names like Mackenzie, Dawson and Hector as if they were his university chums. It kind of got my blood going that he was lecturing us on our mountains, but I did learn that others travelling these trails before us wrote about it, so I'll have to look into it.

We only did about eight miles the first day and today only put in a few, pitching our camp beside the first Bow Lake. Wilcox has said that he wants to move slowly and really enjoy the country, which is alright with me. I think we are both still pretty tired from our Assiniboine exploits and a pleasure trip will be just the medicine the doctor ordered.

August 19
Haven't written for many days because not much of note has happened, but that doesn't mean we haven't been enjoying ourselves. Tonight we are camped at the north end of the Upper Bow Lake in sight of one of the prettiest glaciers I've ever laid eyes on.

For the last few days we've been leisurely exploring the many lakes and glaciers of this wonderland. The only problem has been the cursed river which ran all over the place as we pushed up towards its headwaters, making for some tricky going. The ground reminds me of my morning porridge the way it moves around when the horses step on it. The other day we walked the west side of the Lower Bow

Lake, scrambled up the slopes of the peak on the east side of the valley named after Dr. Hector, and rafted across this lake. Apart from nearly drowning when our raft decided to float a foot under water, things have gone well.

After setting up camp this afternoon I headed off towards the glacier on my own to do a little exploring and fishing. I managed to land a lake trout almost two feet long, so we'll eat well tonight.

August 20
Last night while we were sitting around the fire smoking, drinking cocoa and swapping our usual lies, Wilcox asked me why I always keep my rifle so close and show what he called "imaginary fears" about wild animals, Indians etc. I told him, without worrying too much about the niceties, that he should stick to his own business and leave mine to me. He doesn't seem to appreciate the responsibility I have being in charge of this outfit, and I'm sure he'd be the first to complain to Tom if something got the better of me.

His confounded questions made me more uneasy than usual and during the night I was sure that I could hear the horses telling me there was something on the prowl. I got up twice to check and as I walked through them they seemed pretty calm. But today while W. and I were on the way up to the glacier for some photographs we saw fresh grizzly sign. I went to great pains to point it out to him and think he got the message.

August 23
Bad weather has held us around camp for several days, but

today we headed up into the pass that gives rise to the Bow. It is an interesting place of meadows and gnarled trees, looking like some strange English garden gone wild. When we finally got our first view of the valley of this fork of the Saskatchewan, it was sure a picture. To the west lay a long glacier from the snout of which poured two torrents forming the headwaters of the river. They immediately entered the most fascinating lake I've had the good fortune to lay eyes on. From our lofty perch it appeared to be right at our feet, is large and of irregular shape and contains the most beautiful blue water. Beyond it, down the valley lay a panorama marked by rank after rank of peaks, seeming to stand guard for the secrets that it undoubtedly holds.

We decided to begin exploring these mysteries and started by making the steep descent into the valley. After finding a good campsite by a narrow lake, we have put up for the night, but the weather is acting up again and there's plenty of burnt timber about, so I think I'll take us back up to the pass tomorrow.

August 25
Today I let that damn Wilcox talk me into something I promised to avoid — mountain climbing. I've taken on some high ridges like those going into Assiniboine, but the only real mountain I've ever climbed to the top was Moberly Peak. Jim Wiltshire and I did that back in '87 on a dare when we were near the bottom of a whiskey bottle. I didn't like it then and I don't believe that I enjoy it much better now.

The peak was about 10,000 feet high and located north-east

of our camp on the pass. It started off well because on our approach we ran into some fool hens sitting in tree branches waiting to become supper. I drew down on them and soon had them laying at our feet with their heads knocked off. After hiding them under some rocks to be picked up on our return, we began the ascent proper. It was really just a good walk for most of the way but when we began to get higher up the game began to get a bit more interesting. We got to the top of one of the peaks but the real summit was considerably higher and joined to the one we were on by a long ridge of snow. Wilcox began to knock off the sharp edge of the ridge with his ice axe and told me to follow him up the path he was making. It was too late to turn back, and anyway I wasn't about to let a dude know that a little walk on a ridge at 10,000 feet bothered a trail blazer like me. But the tricky part was soon crossed and we found an easy slope to the top. The view to the north for some seventy-five miles and to the Selkirks in the west for probably 100 was something to behold and made the effort worthwhile. On the way back down I humoured W. by telling him that I now understood what it was that drove him to climb these peaks, and I guess I've got to admit that I wasn't lying.

August 29
We are camped tonight by the banks of the Little Pipestone River with the familiar shape of Mount Temple visible to the south. Tom had convinced Wilcox to take a little detour on the way home to explore the Slate and Sawback Ranges. He had been with the first government surveyors into this area a few years back and he told me the stream to follow comes into the main Bow Valley from the north. I was just about to question his memory when we finally found one just north

of Mount Hector that seemed to fit the bill. The proper route leading over to the Pipestone was not easy to discern, but one trail southward toward Mount Hector showed signs of some former Indian and game use and seemed to hold out some hope. However, it was very steep and barely usable so W. and I spent much of the afternoon rolling stones to create a trail for the horses on a steep cliff portion. I knew Wilcox was worried about all the photographic plates he had exposed getting broken if a mishap should occur, so the next morning I packed them securely on The Bay, knowing he was the most surefooted of the lot. He never missed a step and we were soon over the pass and descending rapidly into a beautiful valley with views of waterfalls cascading down the slopes of Mount Hector to the south. We reached the Pipestone early in the afternoon.

September 5
Unlike the early part of this trip, some of the past few days have been anything but pleasant as both the lay of the land and the elements have turned against us.

Leaving the Pipestone Valley we headed over a divide onto Baker Creek and then up a small side stream right into the heart of the Sawback Range. These peaks are very striking in appearance and we would have had a pleasant stay amongst them except for the confounded weather. Going over a pass into Forty Mile Creek we were hit by a heavy snowfall and the horses hooves began to resemble snowballs, making the going very treacherous. Seeing the landmarks disappearing in the snow and worried that we might lose our way entirely, I decided to take a risk and gallop the horses off the exposed pass. It was mighty scary as they slipped and slid along the trail. Even after we reached the trees it wasn't much better, as the trail descending into the valley was extremely steep and snow-covered.

The next morning was one of the most miserable I've put in on this occupation. Dead timber littered the landscape and we had to make some long and slippery detours or simply chop our way through those blasted logs with freezing hands in soaking wet clothes. Fortunately in the afternoon we reached the top of Edith Pass and the view into the Bow Valley was a welcome sight. Blazes now began to appear and the way was like a bridle path compared to the twisted route we had been following for the last few days. By the time we reached the main valley the snow had completely disappeared and what we had been through just seemed like a bad dream. We proceeded home at the same leisurely pace at which we had set out and arrived today after a journey of twenty-three days and what Wilcox claims was about 175 miles.

Wilcox will be leaving for the east right away because his university courses are due to start any day. Overall for an American he's not a bad type and I hope we see more of his ilk next year. I think this trail business is going to agree with me, but for the next while I'm going to have a closer gander at that Simpson Pass area which looked so interesting when we went through there on our Assiniboine trip.

IV
1896

June 29

Well, I'm back at the old stand ready to take another crack at guiding dudes and hoping it will prove as interesting as last year.

There's been a few changes around here as Tom has taken on some hands to help out on the guiding and packing end. He had some problems while I was out with Wilcox on the Bow last year when he couldn't find a decent guide to take a group of mountaineers from Lake Louise on a little excursion to climb in the region to the north. These men were part of a group of twenty from a Boston club and I guess he wanted to please them, so he agreed to guide them to Mount Hector himself! Only problem was all the horses were out, so they had to trek up there on foot using some poor bugger he had hired to be a human packhorse to carry the grub. The Yanks were not amused, and I guess it convinced Tom that if we're going to get these gents to come back we've got to give them what they want.

It seems too that he wants someone who can talk their language without an English accent because he is stocking up on Americans for the outfit. Two of them, Tom Lusk from Texas and Fred Stephens from Michigan, I just met a few days ago and they seem to know the business end of a cayuse. But I'm not too sure about some of the mere boys I've seen walking around the corrals not knowing a lash rope from a lasso.

Anyway, I hear that Wilcox and Barrett are coming back together for a close look at the country that W. and I began to get into north of Bow Pass last year, and I'm yearning to lay eyes on it again myself.

July 5
Damnation. Wilcox and Barrett are here but Tom just told me that he intends to send Stephens and Lusk out with them. It seems he wants to save me for what he called a more important task — guiding some of the members of the Appalachian Club who had such a difficult time on their trek to Mount Hector last year. They spied Mount Balfour from the summit of Hector and have decided they want to climb it this year. Tom tells me there will be four dudes, Messrs. Abbot, Fay, Thompson and Little, and that they have been writing pestering him about routes to travel, the cost, the number of horses and men etc. etc. He wants nothing to go wrong this year and feels I am the most reliable guide he has available. I guess I should be pleased that he has so much confidence in me, but I would still rather be chopping the way down the little fork with W. and B. than sitting around a campfire waiting for these gents to have their fun.

They intend to begin by making a climb of Mount Lefroy at Lake Louise, which they were unsuccessful at last year, and so it will be early August before we get under way. In the meantime Tom has a few parties lined up for short trips up around Cascade and he wants me to whip the new cayuses he bought from the Stonys into shape on these. There will be some ladies along, and I'm not sure how to make pack horses out of these knotheads without using a bit of trail language. I can hear myself now: "Please get along dear little pony and don't make a fuss so I don't have to take it out of your pretty sorrel hide."

August 4

Bad news! I was just about to set out for Laggan this morning to join Tom and get this Balfour trip started when I received a wire that there's been an accident and to await further instructions. Hope its not too serious.

August 5

Everybody's worst fears from yesterday's news have been confirmed. One of the climbers on Lefroy, Philip Abbot, slipped and fell to his death according to a CPR official who arrived here today. Tom is one of the party trying to recover the body but at last word they had not yet returned to the chalet at the lake. This doesn't bode well for the trip.

August 6

Tom arrived late last night on a freight with Abbot's body. He told me that he and the American gentlemen had experienced a difficult time trying to recover it and only got down yesterday morning after spending a miserable night on Victoria Glacier. There's going to be an inquest so, of course, our trip is cancelled. Don't think I want to hang around here for all the carrying on so I'll probably head out for Simpson Pass and use the time prospecting.

* * *

September 15

My time poking around the rocks has been very productive

and I've gathered a lot of samples from outcroppings near the little lakes standing at the foot of the long ridge by Healy Pass. Some contain a good show of copper and I'm going to get them assayed in Calgary.

I'm back in Banff because Tom wants me to take out a group of American hunters for sheep, goat and grizzly north of Upper Bow Lake. I would just have soon called the year a dead loss from a guiding point-of-view, but he seemed particularly anxious for me take these gents out. And since I missed the opportunity to explore the little fork with Wilcox and Barrett, who apparently had an exciting time, I've agreed. The dudes, who Tom tells me are very important, are two New York financial magnates, a Mr. Peabody, a stockbroker, and a Mr. Barnes, a banker. I can understand why they are so important to Tom but their positions don't cut any ice with me.

September 19
We left Laggan two days ago and after the usual pleasantries of the early going we have been making good time, arriving near the Upper Bow Lake today. This afternoon I decided to try out the gents' marksmanship to see what I could expect when the real shooting began. I set up a few tin cans and told them to sight in their rifles, which they attempted to do with very little success. I made a point about their shortcomings by knocking the targets off the log with my Colt.

Like most Americans, I can't tell them a thing. Peabody decided that he was going to help out by chopping a little wood. I told him not to bother but he took my axe anyway and headed off. I soon heard some strange sounds and went over to investigate. He had found a convenient rock on which to set up the wood and was using it as a confounded chopping block! Grabbing the axe and examining its now dull and chipped edge, I let go with a blast and told him to let me do the work he was paying for. He stalked off back to his tent in a huff and I didn't see him again until supper time. Our evening around the campfire was understandably somewhat uncomfortable.

September 21
Yesterday we crossed over Bow Pass and began making our way through the burnt timber down the little fork. En route we passed by the interesting lake and glacier that Wilcox and I had spied last year at its head. It is rough but very interesting country and today we camped by a couple of lakes that are joined by a narrow neck of land and dominated by a pyramid-shaped peak. Apparently the dudes took me at my word when I said I would prefer to do the work, for when I suggested that we go out spotting for game they told me I could do that while they relaxed. This time I really blew my top and told them that I was not their servant and if there was any game spotting to be done we were all going to do it. That seemed to clear the air and we spent a few good hours glassing for goat on the steep slopes of the aforementioned peak. We didn't spy anything but it looks like prime country and I'm sure we won't have much trouble finding some sport.

September 23
We finally hit paydirt today and tonight I've been skinning out two fine billies around the campfire.

This morning, while the others were finishing breakfast, I began spotting the surrounding peaks and in no time picked out some telltale white specks high up on the pyramid peak. We set off immediately but had to scramble up some pretty steep scree slopes. With my gents slipping and sliding at every step I was certain the goats would have heard our coming. But when we got to a ridge where some boulders offered protection I got out the binoculars and could still see them higher up on some thin ledges.

I was afraid the updrafts might carry our scent to the flock so I very carefully led P. and B. around to the north and up to a good stand near an escape route I thought the goats might take. I then headed back down and around to the south so as to send them in the right direction when they discovered me. It was already past noon when I got in position and began climbing up towards them. Just as I had suspected they began to get anxious and soon headed around the ledge to the northward. A few minutes later I heard a regular fusilade of shooting and then some war whoops indicating success from my dudes.

It took me almost an hour to reach them and I saw that one of the two goats had fallen over a cliff several hundred feet. Now my real work for the day began as I had to haul the one animal back up, gut both and prepare them to be carried into camp. Fortunately, Arthur heard the shooting and brought up a packhorse. After the obligatory photographs of the nimrods with their trophies we loaded them up and got back here about 5 p.m.

September 24

It's funny how success has led to such a change of climate around here. Now Peabody and Barnes are full of compliments and can say nothing bad about the country that they were cursing so roundly only a day or two ago.

We're headed back towards Bow Pass today as their sights have now shifted to bigger game after their success on goat. We're going to head up towards the lakes opposite the glacier that looks like a bird's foot as Tom mentioned that he feels it may be good grizzly country.

V
1897

January 1
New Year's Day and colder than a whore's heart!

I'm at Banff recovering from some of the fun we had bringing in the New Year at the Alberta Hotel last night. A few of
us who worked for Tom last year got together and had a little shindig and now I'm paying the price. I can't let this
town living get too comfortable if I'm going to make it on
the trapline, and I've decided to reform. Tonight I'm going
to take my tarp and sleep down on the river to start tough-
ening up.

January 2
By God, I made it through the night, but just barely. The
thermometer was reading -30 when I hit for the ice last
evening. I piled up a bank of snow to keep the north wind
from biting too deep and made sort of a burrow which I
lined with a big tarp. I rolled into it with my sleeping robe
and could feel the cold from the ice coming up underneath,
but just tried to ignore it by thinking about everyone back
home. They'd probably all think I was crazy if they knew
what I was doing, and I guess they wouldn't be far wrong. I
slept sort of fitfully and a few times had to get up and jump
around a bit to keep the blood running. It was all I could do
to stop myself from hitting out for a warm bed, but I managed to control the urge.

January 3
Slept on the river again last night. This time it wasn't near as

cold — the thermometer was only reading -20 when I headed down there. I slept better but was just about scared out of my longjohns when one of the neighborhood coyotes roaming the riverbank answered a freight with a howl right in my ear. I'm starting to feel like my body is being purged and after a few more nights of this I'll be ready to get back on the line.

* * *

April 14

I'm just back from the Simpson River where we had a very successful spring grizzly hunt. I managed to get two big fellows with prime skins and without much trouble at that. The snow conditions were as good as I've ever seen them and the tracking was pretty easy, so there was no guessing as to where the bear family was looking for their spring breakfast.

Tomorrow I'm going to head up to the Simpson Pass diggings, put away all the traps and begin to do some work. That last assay showed up good and its time to do some real blasting to find out how deep this stuff goes.

April 20

I've spent the last few days getting the cabin in shape before I get serious about the mine. I took the roof off and added a few more rounds of logs for a bit better headroom and put in the new stove and pipe I packed up here — also did some work on the lean-to for storing the saddles and feed. If this thing pans out like I hope it will, I'll have to keep a few head up here to haul out the ore. While the feed will be topnotch around the little lakes in the summer, I'll have to keep some oats to beef things up a bit when the snow's deep.

I was thinking today as I stopped and sat down for a pipe how beautiful this place is. Looking across the valley at Mount Bourgeau from the cabin is just about as fine a vista as is imaginable in these mountains and these groves of larch trees add a beautiful touch. In a couple of months the meadows will be a mass of a million flowers and with the clouds reflecting in the water of the little lakes it will be about as close to Heaven as its possible to be on this Earth.

April 25
This single jacking I've been doing for the past few days is as backbreaking an occupation as is imaginable. I start by coldchiseling a hole in the rock for a charge, put in the powder and cap and let her go. Then the real fun begins as I clear away the debris and put in timber props to try hold the whole thing up. The shaft I'm working goes straight in near the crest of the valley side, but the rock's pretty rotten so I've got to be careful. One mistake and I'm coyote bait because there's sure as Hell nobody knows where I'm at unless they've heard the blasting.

Everything looks good so far. This is the best shaft I've sunk here in the past two years and if I can see that there's a few more feet of ore I'm going to stake. I'll have to go over to the Columbia to register the claim but that's alright. I've been thinking what to call this property and I've settled on "The Bookrest." There's a little hillock that reminds me of one when I look towards the cabin from the small lake to the west of me.

VI
1897

June 29

Tom has asked me to come back with the outfit again this summer, and almost against my better judgment I said I would take another crack at it. After last year's experience I thought that working the claim might be a better bet now that I've made the effort to stake it. But on the other hand, it'll be nice to have some real money in my pockets come fall if I do get a few parties.

The script sounds like one I've heard before — I'll begin by taking a few short trips around Banff in July before hitting the long trail for the north in August with a party that intends to climb Mount Lefroy on August 3rd, the anniversary of Abbot's death. Hopefully the script this year will not turn out to be for a Greek tragedy!

August 8

It's not often a guide loses his dudes before even meeting them, but yesterday was one of those days.

The party I was to take to Mount Balfour was composed of three Americans, Professor Charles Fay, Herschel Parker and Charles S. Thompson of the Appalachian Club, three of my fellow countrymen, Dr. J. Norman Collie, George P. Baker and Professor Harold. B. Dixon of the English Alpine Club and a Swiss climbing guide named Sarbach. With the exception of Baker, who was fresh off the train, this group had already made the ascent of Mount Lefroy and had then followed it up with a climb of Mount Victoria. Tom had suggested that myself and the other men, Lorne Richardson packer and Charlie Black cook, should pull out ahead and get the first camp ready while the gentlemen came down from the chalet, got loaded up and joined us later in the afternoon. I had my doubts but took my orders, leaving three horses for them to load with their remaining baggage.

We pushed through the downed timber and muskeg to the usual first stop, which we not so fondly call "the damp spot and wet place." As we went along I cut some fresh blazes so they could easily find the way through the timber, but there was nothing but our tracks to follow through the blasted muskeg. We pitched camp and waited, but as dark came on I had no doubt that they had experienced some difficulty. Picturing grizzlies chewing on them or their horses sinking in the muck, I decided to build up the fire and let off a few rounds to try give them our position.

About 11 p.m., just when I was beginning to give up hope, Professor Fay dragged his hinders into camp and told me that they had lost the trail and had wandered into a deep muskeg where the cayuses were stuck up to their withers. Getting a bead on their location from Fay, I took my best dog, Mugs, and set out with a lantern into the swamp. It didn't take me long to find them with Mugs' help and they were mighty pleased to make my acquaintance at that point. The cayuses were going nowhere, and I decided to leave them under Mugs' guard while I took care of the dudes. I had them in camp shortly after midnight ravenously devouring one of Charlie's bannocks before rolling them wet and bedraggled into their sleeping robes. Welcome to trail life in the Rockies!

Lorne and I were out at the crack of dawn to rescue the pris-
oners from the muskeg. They were a pretty forlorn looking
bunch, but we soon had the baggage repacked and were on
our way back to camp. While eating breakfast I got to know
my dudes a little better and discussed their plans. There was
some debate as to whether to attack Mount Balfour from the
Upper or Lower Bow Lake, and as the decision was made in
favour of the former we were soon pushing up the valley on
what is now a familiar route.

August 9
I'll be damned if these dudes aren't determined to get themselves into the worst jackpots.

We arrived at the fine camp at the north end of the lake last
evening and today our climbers decided to get right at it.
They broke into two groups, one disappearing around the
side of the Bow Glacier and the other going straight up the
middle before they were lost to our view. Later we learned
that they climbed a peak they supposed to be Mount Balfour
but on getting to the top they saw it was actually further to
the south and should have been approached from Lower
Bow Lake, as I had suspected.

Having some time on their hands they decided to take on
the ascent of a little nub across a snowfield to the westward.
While making their way to it in two groups, Mr. Thompson
fell through a snowbridge and down a crevasse headfirst
and became lodged upside down in the ice some sixty feet
below. Collie bravely volunteered to go down and rescue
him and he was let down on a rope with a foot stirrup made
in the end. After a difficult struggle he managed to get

Thompson turned around and got a second rope on him that was pulled to the surface by his worried comrades. From my understanding of the situation, he was extremely lucky not to have been killed by the fall in the first place and even more fortunate that Collie was able to get him out. That sure would have left me in a fine pickle.

Around the campfire the gents were able to joke about the experience, Thompson saying that henceforth he would confine his scientific investigations to the summits of mountains and leave the depths of icefields to others. While I still don't fully understand what brings them out here, I must admit that these fellows have real sand and are made of good stuff!

August 16

After seeing that Mount Balfour was more accessible from Lower Bow Lake, we moved back down the valley on the 10th. Dixon had to return to Banff to go on to some meeting in Toronto so I sent Richardson to see him back safely. The weather turned sour and the expedition the next day up the icefield flowing from Balfour was turned back. The Americans had made other plans and were anxious to get to Banff so after a brief rest we returned by much the same route we had explored the year before, except that this time we came out by Johnston's Creek to Castle Mountain.

While camped there we visited with one of the mountain's most notable prospectors, Joe Smith. I know Joe well, as I have often visited with him to discuss geology and possible mining ventures. He first came into this country when Silver City was started on this site in '82 on rumours of fabulous finds in the surrounding hills. Joe knows every rock and gully around here and presently is single jacking a prospect near the original Alberta Mine up on Copper Mountain. He had the Englishmen eating out of the palm of his hand with tales of the riches he had discovered, but I know different. There is a mother lode in these mountains but Joe hasn't discovered it yet. I have a pretty good idea the Bookrest may be it.

Today we are back at Laggan and since Collie and Baker still have some time to spend on their "vacation" we are leaving tomorrow to try find a big peak they saw on their climb with Thompson and company. They think it is Mount Murchison, lying to the north of the Waputehks. We'll be leaving from here with pretty much the same outfit.

August 17

I had it out with the bloody Englishmen today. My experience last year with Peabody and Barnes taught me that if there is a burr under my saddle it's better to deal with it head on rather than letting it gnaw away at me and get my dark side going. That way there is no misunderstanding.

We started in weather hotter than a fresh-baked bannock and as the bulldogs and mosquitoes were swarming in clouds that first stretch of trail was even more trying than usual. Everyone's fuse was short and I was concerned about the horses, as I have seen what these conditions can do to a cayuse's hide. I put up at the first good campsite and Collie and Baker told me that they did not want to stop so early and demanded that we continue. I chose to ignore them as I was busy getting the camp set up and taking care of the

horses, but after dinner I gave them my best lecture, informing them that the animals were my first priority and that
they had no idea of how much they were able to do in one
day. I endedwith a peace offering, opining that they should
be able to go much longer once they were in shape and the
heat let up, as I knew it would.

August 19
Damnation if the predictions I made in my little harangue
haven't come true. The heat and the bugs are enough to
drive us crazy and as soon as we reach camp I take the horses to the nearest water to wash them down and rub the cinch
sores with bacon grease to keep the flies off. It helps, but
several ponies are sore and showing signs of blowing up, so
we're going to take a day off at Upper Bow Lake and let
them recover.

Collie has seen the error of his ways and has tried to patch
things up with me. Last evening he engaged me in a conversation about chemistry. He is an interesting study — a
bachelor who devotes his time to teaching and researching
organic chemistry most of the year at University College in
London and climbing in Asia, Europe and now Canada the
rest of the time. I have a book in my library on inorganic
chemistry but what he is talking about is all new to me,
especially his research on what he calls "the effects of high
energy electric discharges on low temperature gasses." Its
almost too much for a mere country lad to understand!

August 20
Our day in camp allowed Mr. Baker to do some work on a
survey to determine the heights of the peaks and passes

around here so that he can put them on a map. It's called a plane table survey and was begun by Mr. Parker during our trip two weeks ago. The principles were explained to me, but mathematics were never my strong suit.

I had told the gentlemen of the view of the headwaters of the little fork valley from north of Bow Pass that I had first seen with Wilcox two years ago. They climbed a rock peak to the north-west of camp to see it and told me they were mighty impressed when they returned. Collie also informed me that they had decided on the first name to be placed on their new map — Peyto Lake, for the beautiful sheet of water that gives rise to the little fork. Quite a compliment!

August 23
I've finally made a close acquaintance with the Saskatchewan River, and its everything the boys have told me, especially after all this hot weather. We had a tough three days making our way down the little fork, or Bear Creek as some call it, spending one night at my camp of last year beside the two lakes which the dudes have named Waterfowl Lakes on their map. There is a deep canyon in the lower reaches of the fork and we had to ford it near its juncture with the main Saskatchewan. Pet, my mare, was pretty uncertain about it because the high water was moving like a freight train and rolling rocks along the bottom, making the footing slippery. The Grey is the best horse in the outfit for this kind of work — he wouldn't be bothered by a stick of dynamite going off in his pack — so I sent Collie across on him first. We're going to camp here and lay over for another day as the horses have lost all their mustard and the hot weather shows no signs of breaking.

There's a large squared-off tree here on which every party that has used this camp before us has carved their initials, so we're going to oblige and do likewise.

August 29
The Englishmen and Sarbach have been having an interesting time this past week climbing the peaks along the Saskatchewan, trying in particular to get to the summit of the one they believe is Mount Murchison near the headwaters. We have been moving the camp up the valley as they do so. Except for the days we move it has been easy going for us and the horses have come back to life.

The first peak they took on just to the west of the confluence of the little fork and the main Saskatchewan they named Sarbach after their guide. I'm not taken with naming a good peak after a climbing guide brought from Switzerland for a few weeks work, but I guess that's their business.

The weather finally started to show its bad side and the climbing and views became somewhat hampered. We moved upstream closer to their prize and while they waited for the snow to melt off the upper slopes we explored the valley leading from a glacier on the branch coming from the southward. The gentlemen climbed part way up another fine peak near the glacier, which they have named Mount Freshfield, and while doing so Collie spied a large peak far away to the north that he believes might be either of the legendary Mounts Hooker or Brown. According to him, a fur trader some years back went through a pass at the headwaters of the Athabasca River and discovered some peaks over 16,000 feet high, naming them after the English botanists

Hooker and Brown. As with Wilcox, I found myself not knowing what my dude was talking about because he had read something that I hadn't. It's beginning to make me damn mad.

September 2
Yesterday we made one last try at bagging Collie's and Baker's peak by guiding them to a camp at its foot up a little valley that comes in from the north. But the weather was wretched and although Collie and Sarbach got part way up, they were turned back by snow showers.

The weather, the late date and a larder that looks like it was meant for a day trip has led us to abandon the attempt for this year. Our plan had been to return to the railroad at Field via the Howse Pass, at the foot of which we are now camped. I recalled for the dudes Tom Wilson's tales of woe about the tough going on the Blaeberry during his trips through there for the railway survey in 1882 and again with some English hunters in 1887. But they would have none of it, and tomorrow we are to take it on, although not without a bit of doubt about our chances of success.

September 4
Just as Tom told me, this is one s.o.b. of a trail. As soon as we crossed the divide the woods became thicker than a porcupine's quills and the downed timber equally as pleasant. The Blaeberry Valley is steep and narrow requiring much slipping and slidding up and down hill. I had to try take the horses over some logs as big as freight wagons as there was no room to outflank them. Our first camp was on little more than a gravel bar and I could count the shoots of grass for

horse feed on my fingers.

Today was hardly better but at least the valley opened up some and just before we camped we came across a deserted trapper's cabin. I've lived the trapper's life myself on occasion so I know how lonely it can be, but I can't imagine why anyone would chose this valley — they must truly hate mankind. After we found a good spot for a camp I went ahead to scout the canyon, which I knew was not far downstream. Tom had told me that it had nearly been the end of him both times through here and my investigation showed that he was telling no tales. I figured that a week of chopping would gain us no more than half a mile and some spots where avalanches had brought down pines were totally impassable. To make it more pleasant I could see that a forest fire was burning in the timber just below. I returned to camp and found that the gentlemen had climbed a bit up the side of the valley and saw a pass in the mountains to the south-east which might hold a way out of this timbered trap.

I'm going to give the canyon one more look tomorrow but if I can't see any way through I'm going to take the chance and try the route Collie and Baker have proposed. I can vaguely recollect someone telling about such a pass in '87 or '88 when I was at Moberly. If it doesn't work we'll have to hit the backtrail, a ten day trip with provisions for less than half that left in the packs.

September 7
Tonight we are camped in fine weather just to the south of the pass that I believe we are the first to cross with horses.

Collie has christened it Baker Pass, and I'm certain it is the only way that animals can be taken from the Columbia to the Blaeberry above the canyon. It was no picnic getting here as the way was steep and as we got higher up there was no water or feed. Snow began to fall before we camped that night but it seemed to clear the air and I can feel Indian Summer on the way. I'm now in more familiar territory and tomorrow we will start following down the north fork of the Kicking Horse to Field.

September 9
We hit Field today and headed for Mount Stephen House for a good square meal, a shave and a bath. There is only one other guest, a Dr. Habel, who has been eyeballing the southern side of the Waputheks with an outfit guided by Fred Stephens, so Collie and Baker immediately started comparing notes with him. They are returning to Banff on the train tomorrow before departing for the east, while Fred and myself will put our strings together and head back in a more leisurely fashion on the tote road.

All in all, I must admit that I have grown to like and respect these two Englishmen, just as I did Wilcox after I got to know him. We've had times when we didn't see eye to eye but they are soon forgotten when we are back home warm and dry. I hope I'll see them again.

VII
1898

March 17

Ran into Tom Wilson today and he told me he's just received a packet from Collie. It seems that after he got back to England he started to do some real investigation into those peaks we saw last year. His curiosity led him to accounts of some of the early fur traders, in particular David Thompson, and to information on David Douglas, the botanist who named Mounts Hooker and Brown. He also put his hands on a copy of Palliser's report, which he has sent to Tom after reading it himself. In his letter he said he intends to return next summer and take up the hunt for the big peak he saw from Mount Freshfield last year, believing that it might be Hooker or Brown.

If I'm going to go in search of these infernal mountains, I'm damn sure I don't want Collie quoting chapter and verse without knowing the text myself, so I asked Tom if I could borrow the Palliser. He said he would pass it on to me after he finished it, but in the meantime he has loaned me a copy of the book that Wilcox has recently had published, so I'll start with it.

March 20

I had a glance at Wilcox's book and found the section he did on the geology of the mountains pretty basic, but the historical section was very interesting. I now understand some of the references he made to people like Sir George Simpson and other fur traders. He briefly mentions the work of the Palliser Expedition and in particular Sir James Hector, who

Mount Hector is named after. He looks like a man after my own heart, and today Tom brought the Palliser over to me, so I'm going to put the Wilcox aside and get right to the original.

March 22
Once I got going on Palliser I couldn't put it down and spent all day reading in front of the fire. This Hector was an amazing fellow and deserves all the credit our dudes give him. He knew his geology and his powers of observation were of a high order — he even saw things in some of the territory he travelled that I have missed myself. He sure covered a lot of ground and put many names on the features around here. One interesting point I learned — the peak Collie and Baker were wanting to climb that they thought was Mount Murchison is actually Mount Forbes. Mount Murchison is the peak that stands immediately east of the junction of the little fork and the Saskatchewan.

I should be able to hold up my side of the confab with Collie now!

* * *

July 31
Collie stepped off the train at Laggan today with some new climbing friends, Hugh Stutfield and Hermann Woolley, and thankfully no Swiss guides. Bill Byers will be in charge of the bannock and Nigel Vavasour and Roy Douglas will pack and take care of the thirteen horses, all Tom could spare. Our aim is to determine if the peak Collie saw last year was either Mount Hooker or Brown, but the

Englishmen also stated they are interested in extending the
plane table survey for mapmaking purposes, climbing any
new big peaks we might discover and investigating the
sources of the Saskatchewan, Athabasca and Columbia
rivers as time allows. It sure sounds good to me.

We headed up the valley of the Pipestone, new territory but
the route we have chosen so Collie can investigate the real
Mount Murchison, which according to Hector is 13,500 feet
high. As neither Stutfield or Woolley had any experience
with downed timber or Indian cayuses, I took care to provide a bit of instruction. Apparently I should have been
more attentive to the pack horses as one of our new recruits
fell and broke its leg while jumping over a log. I had to take
it aside and put it out of its misery and this will make an
already bad situation for the packing even worse. The gentlemen, who are walking the first part of the trip due to the
shortage of horseflesh, may have to do so longer than we
figured.

August 6
Today we arrived at the Saskatchewan after a week spent
going up the Pipestone, across the pass and down the
Siffleur. One of the party, Stutfield, has been quite ill to his
stomach and blames it on Bill's cooking. It's the normal trail
fare — bannock, tea, fried onions and fat bacon — and I've
seen this before when a new dude has to adjust from the
more high-toned menus of the hotels. His discomfort has
been increased by hot weather, flies and lots of thunderstorms which keep everything damp. We are trying out an
Indian teepee instead of the normal fly tents this year, and
while it's more roomy and comfortable, when it rains hard

the water comes down the smoke hole at the top.

We've now fed Stutfield a few doses of epsom salts and the constitution of his stomach seems to rallying to the cause. The way has been new and interesting and the pass very high and desolate (the gentlemen say it is 8400 feet) but as we got into the lower reaches of the Siffleur the going got hot. We made slow time, as the company continued to walk, and every time we forded the stream I had to take them over one at a time on Pet. The trail became a mean one, a tangle of downed timber and muskeg, and it took me and the boys many hours to chop it out while the gentlemen sat and smoked their pipes. Eventually we hit the main valley of the Saskatchewan and the fabled Kootenay Plains, a fine bit of horse pasture and the place where the oldtimers say the Indians used to come over the divide to trade. Tom has spoken often about this open country and I can see why he gets excited about it as a good winter grazing area. We didn't see any of the Stonys he says frequent this place, but we didn't see any game either so they must be around somewhere.

On the north side the valley is filled by a large glacier-crowned peak that Collie has named in Tom's honour. Forming the other side of the valley's portal is Mount Murchison, flattopped and very grand but certainly not as high as Hector made it out to be. While I found the view interesting, I was more concerned with the smoke drifting in from the country to the north where we intend to go. If that wasn't worry enough, one look at the raging torrent at our feet would make anyone consider their future. I didn't say anything but after we camped tonight I studied it hard and can see we're going to have some fun in the days ahead.

August 7
As I expected, today was not pleasant.

The river was tearing away its banks like a dog taking meat
off a bone and in several places the trail was completely
under water. Because it was hotter than blazes the cayuses
were not wont to avoid the many bathing spots. Nitchi
slipped into one bad hole and swam in the wrong direction
to an island in mid-steam. Molly, the bell-mare, followed
with her colt and the little fellow nearly drowned as he was
rolled over and over in the swift current. Despite the fact it
was Sunday, I let forth a torrent of curses that made the
Englishmen cringe and I suggested they continue along out
of earshot while I addressed the situation in the language it
deserved. I swam Pet out into the flood and as the water
came up over the saddle I slipped out and hung onto the
pommel for all I was worth as she battled gamely against
the flow. We made it, but just, and I had to whack the tar out
of those cayuses to get them back across and on their way.

Camp had to be made quickly to dry out the bacon, flour
and sugar from the soaking packs or we would lose all of it,
and with it our chances of reaching our goal. We pitched
camp beside a marsh alive with mosquitoes and finished the
day under general attack.

August 15
We've just completed four exhausting days on the business
end of our axes attempting to cut our way up the north fork
of the Saskatchewan. I've been so tuckered out that I haven't
had the heart to write. Last night we didn't even have the
salt to put up the teepee and just threw our sleeping robes

down around the fire.

Our problem resulted from having to go far upstream on the Saskatchewan to ford, leaving us on the wrong side of the north fork. I was afraid to try crossing the rampaging flood to the east side, requiring us to play beaver on the heavy bush. This morning Nigel and I went ahead to see what the day held, and, as I had feared, we ran into a major stream coming in from the west. When we got back to camp I was pretty down-in-the-mouth and told the Englishmen I didn't like our chances. Collie attempted to cheer me up and brought out a bottle of whiskey to fortify his view. After a few shots I started to feel more optimistic and agreed to try ford the north fork. To my amazement it wasn't as bad as I had imagined. The dudes were now mounted, as we had cached some of our supplies at the mouth of the little fork, and they performed admirably in the swift current. Once on the east side the going was better and after passing the tributary we could take our pick on which side to travel.

Except for the lack of game to fill out the larder, matters are now looking considerably brighter.

August 17
Compared to the previous sixteen, the past few days travelling up the north fork have been pretty easy. At its head we took the trail to the right and then followed a fork to the left to reach a high alpine meadow with a view of a very high peak with an impressive glacier winding its way to the valley bottom. The gentlemen have named them Athabasca Peak and Glacier, and we will have them as companions as we are setting up a headquarters camp here. This is

undoubtedly the same camp that Fred Stephens and Tom Lusk told me they had frequented with Wilcox during their outing last year.

Last night in camp we had a most humourous incident. We had gone to sleep around the fire without the teepee and towards midnight I heard the sound of a large animal moving about in the bush. A cold chill went down my spine as I always worry about grizzlies sneaking up on camp in search of plunder. I woke the boys and quietly told them what was afoot and, armed with our guns and axes, we lit a lantern and headed out in pursuit. We plunged into the bush ready to do battle and there in the lantern light was one very surprised Woolley changing his photographic plates! Lowering our weapons, we roared with laughter, and he looked mighty sheepish. The uproar woke the other dudes and when questioned on returning to camp I told them we had been bear hunting.

While our camp tonight is both picturesque and comfortable, after dinner we did a check of the supplies and were shocked by just how short the rations are. Collie and Woolley are going to start climbing but the rest of us, including Stutfield, are going hunting.

August 23
The gentlemen have made some interesting geographic discoveries during the past week. While the location of Mounts Hooker and Brown has eluded them, they feel they have discovered a big new icefield that sends its meltwaters to three oceans through three separate rivers, the Saskatchewan, the Athabasca and the Columbia.

On the 18th Collie and Woolley climbed Peak Athabasca encountering this icefield stretching as far as the eye could see and viewed the peaks that Collie had seen from Freshfield last year just to the north. The rest of us were involved with the more immediate concern of finding sheep and we set off to the northward, around the pass and peak that Collie has named after Wilcox. I went off to scout around the base of the peak while Nigel and Stutfield took the area more toward the pass, and, as it turned out, the sheep. They spotted a flock of about twenty around noon and spent all afternoon stalking them. Stutfield was no slouch with a rifle when he got the opportunity for he managed to wound three animals, two of which Nigel finished off with his pistol. I was mighty glad of the news when they got to camp and was even more relieved when Collie and Woolley returned long overdue late that night.

The next few days were spent in retrieving the game Stutfield had shot and making some pemmican out of the meat. The gentlemen attempted one of the big peaks to the north they had seen on the 18th and further explored the icefield. Unfortunately they have discovered there is no pass between the two peaks and therefore they cannot be Hooker or Brown. Athabasca Pass still lays further to the north and we will leave the main camp here and begin to scout for it with a smaller outfit tomorrow.

August 30
I'm sitting next to the fire in the teepee writing this with a fierce rain rain pelting down. We're in full retreat down the north fork and have only put up today because of the weather. We have only a few pieces of bread and some

canned sardines left to eat, the last of the dried meat having been finished yesterday. Everybody is looking mighty glum.

Our trip over to the Athabasca was shortlived. The gentlemen did a little climb on a peak they have named Mount Diadem, but they were plagued by thunderstorms and from their lofty perch the country to the north looked inhospitable and not likely to hold any game. That made the decision to head back easy. Once we got back to the main camp I found that some of the mutton had gone bad, making the need to return to our cache at the mouth of the little fork the main order of business.

Stutfield and I pushed on ahead of the packtrain to try bag some game in a valley to the eastward visited by Nigel and Roy on our way out. It is called the Brazeau and they said it looked to be good game country. On our way up the tributary we found the smouldering remains of a fire which could have become a major conflagration had it not been for the recent rains. I suspected Nigel and Roy and they later confirmed they had lit a fire to cook a fool hen they had killed. I gave them both barrels for their stupidity, for if the fire had got away it could well have filled the main valley and blocked our return. Stutfield and I continued over the pass onto the upper Brazeau and I saw enough to reckon it would be a good sheep country before being driven back empty-handed by more rain.

We are still a long distance back to the mouth of Bear Creek, in fact it took us five days to come this far up the other side. We'll have to do better going back down or we'll soon be eating our boots.

September 2
We're camped back at the cache with full stomachs and have spent that last couple of days relaxing and hunting for fool hens, which seem to abound in this area.

The trip back down the north fork was one of the longest days we've ever spent on the trail, but it had to be done. To keep their spirits up, I joked with the dudes about Indians having found our grub and painted a picture of them feasting on our bacon and drinking our whiskey. I kept my fears that this might truly have happened to myself. However, the cache was safe and sound and we went at it pretty good, overindulging and necessitating a two day layover while our digestive systems recover.

Today the gentlemen attempted Mount Murchison but were turned back by snow showers and poor visibility. They made an interesting discovery of a petrified forest high up on its slopes — sometime I'll have to return and investigate it myself.

September 9
Home at last and none too soon.

Our trip down the Bow was no more enjoyable than that down the Saskatchewan due to short commons, unusually cold weather and that damned burnt timber in the last stretch before Laggan. The dudes were determined to get lost, going off to take photographs or whatever, and I had to spend valuable time getting them back on the straight and narrow. When we pulled into the station late this afternoon Collie commented that we looked like chimney sweeps, and

I guess he wasn't far wrong. As the gentlemen got on the late train, they pronounced themselves very happy with the results of the trip, in particular their icefield discovery, and said they hoped to return again.

It's as certain to me as night follows day that these trips on the long trail demand more planning than Tom's been giving them. It's just not possible to gain the farther reaches of this country without enough horses and grub. Tom seems to feel that we can rely on game gathered along the way, but if our recent outing is any indication it's a poor hope indeed.

VIII
1898

October 8

After a few days down at the ranch I had just returned today to get my trapping gear together when I got word that Tom wanted to see me. I wandered down to his corrals on Buffalo Street and found him with Wilcox, who I was surprised to see as he had been suffering from typhoid this summer. Tom explained that he had now recovered and had decided to try fit in a late season trip to explore the headwaters of the Saskatchewan. All the other guides were out with hunting parties and Tom suggested that since I knew the country well, having gone through there last year with Collie's party, I would be the logical choice to accompany him. I said straight out that I thought it somewhat foolhardy to take on that country on a pleasure trip this late in the year, particularly since the fall had been so backward, and that I was anxious to get ready for the trapline. My reasoning didn't seem to impress him greatly and his line of conversation indicated that he felt I owed him a few favours. I didn't take too kindly to his remarks but held my temper. At that point Wilcox began to recount the reasons why he felt I was the best guide in the mountains and I guess he got to my sense of pride because, against my better judgment, I agreed to take him.

October 11

Roy Douglas, Wilcox and I along with nine horses are at Laggan tonight getting ready for the start of our trip tomorrow. There has been snow showers and a driving wind all day, leading me to question more than ever our intelligence in taking this hairbrained outing on. But I've never backed down on my word yet and I'm not about to start now, so its Hell-bent for the North Pole in the morning.

As I recorded our trip over this same ground with Collie last year in some detail, I've decided not to keep the journal up for this one. It'll probably be too cold to get my fingers to write anyway.

October 26
My prediction of October 11th proved altogether too true as the last two weeks have been amongst the most miserable I've put in on the trail because of the pure cussedness of the weather.

For our first three days it was a constant forced march through snow showers to get to the Saskatchewan and we were only just started down the little fork when the real heavy stuff appeared. On the third night it snowed almost a foot, nearly collapsing the tent and requiring a day's lay-over. I had to hike through heavy drifts twice that day to look out for the welfare of the horses, who were pastured about a mile away from camp, and I could easily have used a pair of snowshoes. The next few days were cold and slippery and the packmantles and ropes were constantly frozen, making everything take twice as long to do and almost freezing off our fingers in the process. It took us six days to reach the Saskatchewan.

Fortunately things improved a bit after that and as we turned up the middle fork towards the area around Glacier Lake, which was Wilcox's objective on this trip, the sun even began to shine. The only good thing about the conditions was that the river was so low it could be forded on foot, making our various crossings much easier than usual. Wilcox attempted to climb a small peak to the east of the lake to get a view of Mount Forbes. To get him started and keep him dry I carried him across the outlet stream from the lake on my back. He succeeded in getting up this peak and taking some photographs of Mount Forbes from the summit, although he was almost blinded by the glare of the sun on the new snow.

The weather began to turn sour again and Wilcox indicated he was satisfied with the work he had done, so we set out for Howse Pass and the Blaeberry on the 20th. If anything the conditions were worse than when I went through with the Collie party last year, the snow making the steep valley sides very slippery. Many times the horses had to slide down on their haunches for forty or fifty feet, jump into the stream to cross it and then ascend a similar distance on the other side. At any moment I expected a wreck, and it was more luck than good management that we didn't have a few broken legs in the bunch. Such is the nature of this valley that I could not even discern last year's trail and had to walk most of the way to find the safest route.

When we got further down and turned to go up to Baker Pass matters became even worse. For the first time I really began to fear if we would make it without freezing to death, but had to put on a brave face so Wilcox wouldn't realize the seriousness of our situation. Because of constant snow, we had to use a compass for bearings and as dusk came on I could find no suitable feed in the snow and had to turn the horses loose to fend for themselves while we pitched a makeshift camp. Next morning there was eighteen inches of new stuff and it took me half the day to find the animals and get them packed in the terrible conditions. Again that day we had no guide except the compass and the general slope of the mountain. Our route was constantly crossed by steep-banked gullies and to make matters worse, I couldn't recognize any of last year's landmarks in the deep snow.

We had to resort to going ahead of the horses to break a trail for them, and as they waited they began to lay down in the snow and make pitiful sounds. They had not grazed well for several days and had become weak and affected by the cold. I managed to whack them back to their feet and then forced them on, as there was no choice in the matter. At length the slope became more gentle and I could begin to see the familiar shape of the pass through the clouds. We had to camp on its summit in three feet of snow, but there was good grass underneath and the cayuses pawed through and got a passable feed overnight. As we camped the sun began to break through and lifted our spirits greatly. It was the beginning of a spell of better weather and in three days of careful travelling we arrived at Field, where amazingly there was no snow at all and it was still Indian Summer instead of the deep winter of the heights above.

I've always been one to place a lot of store in my hunches about things and the more I learn about these mountains and the dangers they can hold the more I know I should pay attention to these feelings. This little trip tempting the Winter Gods sure as Hell will make me pay heed to my premonitions in the future.

IX
1898-99

October 28
Earlier this fall I was talking with Jim Simpson — he's a young countryman from Lincolnshire who stumbled into my tent at Laggan two years ago looking like a lost school-boy. He travelled down south a bit sowing his wild oats and last year went to work for our outfit as a cook and packer. He's started to learn the ropes and told me he was dead set on doing some trapping this winter. In a weak moment I said that I had my eye on some of that marten country on the Saskatchewan and that if he wanted he could join me. I've managed to get a few dollars ahead and my old friend Dave White, who has gone into the merchandising business, agreed to grubstake us with supplies from his new store.

October 30
Jim and I got to Laggan yesterday and have camped near the junction of the Pipestone and Bow in order to sort our-selves out before heading up the Pipestone for the pass. I've only been up this valley once but I got a pretty good idea of the lay of the land and know that it is a lot quicker to go this way than by the Bow. Tom agreed to lend me a few of his ponies so I'm going to ride Pinto and Jim The Bay and we'll take a couple of others to carry the freight.

October 31
I'm writing this with numb fingers and the stub of a pencil while we huddle around a fire trying to keep from freezing to death. I'm still learning how this country can turn on you just when you think you got it figured. It's plumb amazing

how often I have to face its twists and turns before I realize that if you don't take it seriously it can kill you. Can't see or feel to write more now so I'll have to wait till we hit warmer climes and better times.

November 2
Am now back at Laggan where Jim and I have returned to thaw out and regroup.

When we left three days ago it was in the fine Indian Summer conditions that had returned after my Howse Pass exploits and we were not really prepared for what lay ahead. As we pushed our way up the river toward the summit we began encountering snow in the valley, but did not give it much thought. That was a mistake as the Pipestone Pass is one of the highest in these parts and well above timberline. We reckoned we could easily get over it that day but as we got higher and it got later in the afternoon it started to snow. Before long it was snowing harder than I can remember and there we were out in the open like fish out of water. Luckily I had brought a shovel and was soon hard at work on the business end trying to cut a trail for the horses through the growing drifts. Some were already five feet deep and the path was blowing in behind us before we had gone a hundred yards. As neither of us knew exactly where the summit lay there was nothing for it but to turn tail and run. Jim couldn't see the trail any better than I and we knew there was only one thing we could do — give the horses their heads and leave it to them to find the way. They took us right back here in two days of hard travelling in bad conditions. As usual they're a lot smarter than two so-called mountain men.

We're going to let things settle down a bit and then head up the Bow — older and wiser again!

* * *

November 17
Jim and I are now near the mouth of Bear Creek building a rough cabin for our winter's activities. We packed in some rolls of tar-paper, a few laths, a stove and pipe, some cooking and eating utensils, a toboggan and snowshoes and twelve dozen sets of various sizes to get ourselves going. We dug down a few feet in a soft spot and are now putting up some rounds of logs before splitting a few of the big fellows to be hauled on as a roof. We'll use the laths to cover the larger openings and try to find a little unfrozen mud and moss in the river for chinking. The tar-paper will be used on the roof to keep us dry. It'll be a little rough but will serve for the time being until we can find out if this country's worth the effort. All this should have been done weeks ago, but our misadventure set us back badly. Fortunately the weather has settled down of late so I'm hoping to get the horses over to their winter pasture on the Kootenay Plains before it closes in for good.

November 26
Arrived back at the cabin today after taking the horses out. I found a fine protected place for them just downstream about a day's travel. It finally started snowing on my return and before reaching here I had to put on the snowshoes for the first time. It'll take a heap more settling before its ready for setting out the traps, but there's lots to do in the mean-

time. Jim spent a little time with one of the old trappers at Lake Louise a few years ago, so he knows the rudiments of the game and is a quick study. He's spent the time getting our stuff sorted out and doing a bit of meat hunting. We'll need some game to go with our bacon and bannock and to use as bait in the traps, so we'll have to concentrate on that for the next little while.

December 1
It's been snowing hard for the past few days and has turned miserably cold, making the meat hunting difficult but getting everything shipshape for the trapline. We were fortunate to get a sheep right away on the slopes of the big peak across the river Collie named for Tom. Today we killed a coyote down by the river, and Jim is in the process of skinning him out in front of the stove as I write this. We have prepared about fifty strychnine caps that we will hide in the meat and scatter about to try bring in some of his brethren — fortunately coyotes aren't too particular about feeding on their own kind.

Mainly we're here for the marten — I saw plenty of sign during the last two summers in this area. We'll run one line back up the river towards Bow Pass and the other up the Saskatchewan to the north and, perhaps, into a few of the side valleys. But we'll be happy to take the odd coyote pelt as well, since they're fetching good prices on the market at the moment and are much in demand. If we have the time we'll probably set out a few snares for lynx, but those polecats are real smart and I've never had a lot of luck with that method.

December 9
I'm writing this piece laying down on my bunk to avoid choking on the smoke. We put this place together in an awful hurry and the stove doesn't draw quite properly — smoke comes back down the pipe whenever it blows hard, as its doing tonight. Jim's laying on his bedroll too, trying to read a copy of Tidbits in the candlelight and haze. We've only been here a few weeks and I think we've read those stories three or four times now. Both of us like to pass the long evening hours reading when we're not too tired, so we'll have to beef up the library the next time we're in town.

We've got the south line laid out now and it wasn't easy. We carried the traps on the toboggan, but because of the snow conditions and the cold it was a battle all the way. Trying to put up the marten sets in the hollows of trees and little nooks and crannies was difficult because our fingers kept freezing up. We also had to build a couple of wickiups for overnight shelter along the way and stock them with the essentials of survival in case we get caught in bad conditions and have to lay over. But we're pleased with our work and after putting out a few snares closer to our headquarters I'm going to lay out the north line while Jim gets to work tending the south.

We got a coyote that took the poison bait and though we had to track him for quite awhile before he dropped, it was worth it as he already has a good early season coat.

December 15
I put in the northern line this past week and only returned to the main cabin today. The weather was bitterly cold and

the going hard, as I mostly used nothing but a little silk tent I carried for shelter. At night the trees were popping and cracking like rifle shots in the cold, so I haven't got much rest. But the country looks good and its interesting to travel under different conditions than I saw this summer.

When I returned here I found that during my absence Jim had taken in only one marten and had lost a coyote, which had chewed off its leg in a trap. That's a damn poor record and Jim said he was thinking about going back to Banff for Christmas and bringing in a few more things after the festive season. I think I'll tag along as I've spent a Christmas in the woods before and its a mite lonely even for someone who can go for months without company.

December 23
We're back in Banff tonight with our tails between our legs again. Jim and I sure are having a disagreement with Mother Nature this year and we're lucky that we didn't lose some of our parts.

We planned on getting to Laggan in two long days and when we set out early three days ago it was cold and clear. We made good time on our snowshoes to Waterfowl Lakes and hoped to make Upper Bow Lake the first night, but as the day wore on the weather turned foul and we had to put up north of Bow Pass. The snow came down so thick we could hardly breathe on the last leg and we had a hard time finding the little wickiup that I knew was just off the trail. We were considering digging a tunnel in the snow just when Jim saw it in one of the brief moments when the blizzard let up. We got a fire going and cooked a bannock so small it barely passed my tonsils going down and then brewed some tea, but that was all we could muster before we rolled into our sleeping robes and passed out from exhaustion.

The next day was a real humdinger and we couldn't move from our lair or we would have quickly perished. Its amazing the thoughts that go through one's mind when you sit for hours on end looking into the swirling snow — I imagine its a lot like the spells those fakirs put on people at the fair. When not thus occupied I instructed Jim in the finer arts of snowshoe repair, as both our footwear was worse for wear from recent experience. I always carry some goatskin from which the hair has been removed for this purpose, because its tough and the snow doesn't ball up in the openings as with babiche. As the day wore on our shelter began to look more like the snow tunnel we had been considering digging. But then the snow miraculously began to let up and we knew that come morning we had to get out no matter what as our food was down to a couple of puny hardtack biscuits.

Today we set out before dawn and had to plough our way through some tremendous drifts that were being whipped by a biting wind, but fortunately it was from the north and we had it in our backs most of the day. We pressed on for many hours without stopping and were a mile or so north of Laggan and plumb tuckered out when we heard the whistle of the train pulling into the station. That put some new life into us and we had to hump it like we were in a snowshoe race down the hill. We got to the station just in time to bang on the side of the car and get the conductor's attention before it pulled out. As soon as we got on the car and the heat hit us, we both passed out and the conductor had to shake us hard to wake us up when we got to Banff.

When I stop and cogitate on it, it sure has been some two months of wear and tear on our hides for a couple of skins, but I guess it beats starving or dying of boredom in town.

* * *

March 15
I just got back today from a little expedition over to see how the horses are faring. It took me awhile to find them because they had taken to a small ravine on the north side of the river to get protection from the weather and to hide from the wolves and coyotes. I found only three sets of tracks and realized that one of them must have become wolf bait in the last few weeks. Before long I found what was left of the frozen carcass of the grey mare and cut off a good piece to use to bait our traps. I followed the tracks of the others to their hideout and found them in good condition considering the cold weather we've been having, but I'm sure going to hate to have to make up for the one to Tom.

Jim is off in Banff to pick up some supplies, new reading material and our mail. He'll cover the southern line on his way in, so I'll be off on the north leg tomorrow. The weather has been exceptionally fine the last few days and I'm hoping it's the first sign of spring.

March 21
I returned from the line today with our best take yet. With the warmer weather the marten have become more active

and my traps yielded three prime pelts. Several other baits had been taken without tripping the mechanism, so I've been on the go from dawn to dark rebaiting and moving some of the sets. On the way back I had a devil of a time hauling the toboggan because of the changing snow conditions. Even though I had just waxed the runners with paraffin I can see that we won't be able to use it much longer.

Jim was here when I arrived, having pulled in two days ago. He was pleased as well because he had found a fine coyote in one of our traps and a lynx, our first, in one of the snares. He told me all the news from Banff, which took about two minutes, and we then began laying plans for the next few weeks as we stretched the new pelts. With spring coming on, the bears will be stirring soon and we'll get out a couple of bear traps we have and start preparing for bigger game.

X
1899

September 23
On coming in off the trail last week I met an Australian
bloke, Jack Sinclair, who knows more about minerals and
prospecting than anyone I've ever had the good fortune to
run across. He turned up one evening in the King Edward
bar and I heard him mention he was here to do some
prospecting, so I offered to buy him a whiskey and struck
up a conversation. He told me that some time back he'd
been on the gold hunt in New Guinea with about twelve of
his countrymen, but they'd had some troubles with the
natives, the wild animals and the rivers and he was only one
of two who lived to tell the tale. More recently he's been in
the Klondike, but feels there's so many rushing in to stake
there who know nothing about mining that the whole thing
is a mess. He did stake a few claims with some partners but
became so disgusted he left. His knowledge is great, so we
had much to talk about.

September 29
There's not many people I'd confide in about my prospecting and claims, but Jack Sinclair is one of them. I've asked
him his opinion of the Bookrest and today we came up here
so he could eyeball it. He says that from his limited experience with copper it looks like its got what it takes to make a
going proposition, and he offered me some helpful advice.

I showed him my copy of Dr. Dawson's 1884 report on the
geology of the Rockies and he found it highly interesting.
We agreed that the stratigraphy and minerals he described

in the mines on Copper Mountain were very similar to what we see here and that these deposits are undoubtedly an extension of the same formation. Dawson says that R. G. McConnell did some geological work up here in 1885, so it might be useful to see if we can find any reports.

September 30

Jack and I got into the whiskey last night and began hatching all kinds of schemes for prospecting and mining around here. In the end I offered to take him in on this prospect, because its become obvious that working it would be much more productive with two men than one. He happily agreed and promised to find some other ground which we could partner on that would pay me back for my generosity. He's also got his eye on a lot down in Banff along the river and suggested that we build something on it together. I'm getting a mite tired of bunking in at the Red Onion the little I'm in town, so I just may agree.

XI
1900-01

January 28

Jack and I were sitting in the shack tonight jawing about the war and reading the Calgary newspaper. In it was the welcome news that Lord Strathcona has agreed to foot the bill for the raising of a contingent to fight the Boers in South Africa. It is to be under the command of Colonel Sam Steele, well known in these parts for his work in charge of the North West Mounted Police during construction days. It will be manned by a special corps of mounted riflemen recruited in the west with the officers and NCOs coming from the Mounted Police.

While I would never leave these mountains for the mother country, I have to admit that the old loyalties still run strong in my veins at times like this. Jack, although born in Australia, has been equally moved, and after a few whiskeys our blood really got boiling and we decided that one of us should join up while the other takes care of our claims. We agreed that the only fair way to decide was to flip a coin, and I won! Tomorrow I'm going down to the police barracks and put my name forward.

February 1

Things have been moving fast on this Lord Strathcona business. I've just got off the train after making my pilgrimage to the recruiting office in Calgary. They're going to split the unit between Manitoba, the North West Territories and British Columbia, so there will be less than two hundred men from each. The competition is tough — the recruiting officer told me that they've had four times as many men as they can use come forward. After talking with me about my experience with horses and hearing the tale of some of the jackpots I've been able to extricate myself from over the past few years, he said I pretty much fit the bill. I expect to hear one way or the other within the next few days.

February 3

I received a wire today that Steele has made his choice and I'm in! Many other Banff boys tried but as far as I know only two others have made the grade, Louis McCallum and Bill Saddington. We don't have much time to get prepared because we have to be in Calgary ready to move out for the east on the 5th. We had to agree to sign up for a year, so I won't be seeing these hills again for quite a spell. Hopefully I'll make it back with my hide intact.

February 14

It's been quite an experience since I last wrote.

On the 8th we boarded a special train leaving from Calgary, joining the boys in B Squadron coming from British Columbia. As we headed east more joined in at every stop and crowds of people gathered to cheer us as we passed through the towns and villages. The boys are a rough and ready lot, many having busted broncs on cattle ranches, and each has his own stories to tell. Mine are a bit different and I have been pestered every night to give the newly-joined some of the details of my mountain trips. It reminded me of some of the evenings spent entertaining the dudes around the campfire, but the audience is certainly more unruly.

Early today we reached Ottawa and immediately marched to Lansdowne Park where we are to be billeted. The barracks are in an old stable and come complete with straw mattresses. When we arrived they were already bringing in some of our mounts, tough ranch-bred stock that looks like it will need some work but should be able to go the distance. In the afternoon we were issued with our uniforms and gear. The uniforms are stiff and uncomfortable, like they've been made out of packmantles, but the rest of the issue looks pretty good. Each of us was given a high-pommeled stock saddle complete with a lasso, a revolver and a good Lee Enfield rifle. Our headgear resembles the stiff brimmed stetsons of the Mounted Police that some of the Banff boys wear for mountain use.

March 6

I now know how an unbroken cayuse feels after I've worked him hard because we've been training morning, noon and night for the last three weeks. I've been so played out that I haven't had the ambition to write. I've got to admit we had some pretty rough edges when we got here, and the horses were about the same. But the effort has been paying off and we now know the basic formations and can get the horses to perform them.

Today Steele showed us off in front of the Governor General, Lord Minto. Considering that the snow was knee deep and the space was limited the best we could do was pass by in our sections of fours, but everybody felt pretty good about our performance.

March 17

Since leaving Ottawa we have been greeted by large crowds and hailed wherever we go. Five days ago there was a tremendous banquet held for us at Windsor Hall in Montreal with the mayor and all of the dignitaries there. While the thought was nice, it reminds me of why I left England and prefer my secret places in the mountains where I can escape all this. I already miss them more than I could have imagined.

When we left the banquet we marched through a crowd that the newspaper estimated at 30,000 to reach Bonaventure Station. We proceeded through New Brunswick and on to Halifax where another huge crowd greeted us today as we boarded our vessel, the S. S. Monterey of the Elder Dempster line, chartered by Lord Strathcona for our personal use. When we boarded there were 28 officers, 512 men and 599 horses, so there's quite a boat full.

March 28

When I could see how miserable this voyage was going to be I decided not to record the details every day. But for the record I do want to give a picture of what's been happening.

This tub has been tossing around like a cork even though the sea is not that rough and most of the prairie boys have never experienced anything like it before so they're suffering terribly. I'm spending part of my time trying to take care of some of the worst cases of seasickness and much of the rest on the detail for horse disposal. A few days out one of the horses developed pneumonia and now its running rampant through the whole bunch in these close quarters. Every day now for several we've had to dump the carcasses of five or six overboard for fishbait and it gives no sign of stopping. When not engaged in either of these two unpleasant pursuits, the Colonel has managed to organize some decent weapons training and drill exercises that will serve us well when we go into action.

April 10

Today we arrived in Table Bay and disembarked in Cape Town. The trip continued pretty much as I wrote last time, and we have lost over 170 horses to the epidemic that ran through them. One wag in our outfit summed it up pretty well when he said "I guess we'll be Strathcona's Foot by the time we get to South Africa."

Colonel Steele is now awaiting his orders as to where and when we shall get our first crack at the Boers. I will now have to discontinue this journal as one of the officers informed me that any written information about our movements could fall into enemy hands and journals or letters of any but the most general kind are now disallowed.

* * *

January 20

Today we arrived back at Cape Town and embarked immediately for our voyage to England. We were told that we were now free to take up any letter or journal writing we wished, and as soon as I got out of the rags left of my uniform and into the new togs sent to us by Lord Strathcona I decided to begin the task. While I don't have the stomach to write the details of some of the things that have happened over the past nine months, I do want to record the main points so that I will always be able to recall them.

We began our service here with an exercise that was typical of the blunders that the British had been guilty of in this war up until the time of our arrival. The objective was to penetrate deep behind enemy lines with the intention of severing the Boers' supply line by blowing up a railway bridge on the line between Pretoria and Delagoa Bay. We moved into position to do so on two occasions but at the last moment the plan was called off because the false intelligence reports planted by the Boers fooled the British generals into thinking the enemy was on to them.

Consequently it was not until late June after a forced march that we joined General Sir Redvers Buller's Natal Field Force on the Natal-Transvaal border and became part of Major General Lord Dundonald's 3rd Mounted Brigade advancing along the Natal Railway towards Johannesburg. Our first contact with the enemy occurred on July 1st when we were fired on from two farmhouses flying white flags, and although we killed four Boers we also lost one man killed and two taken prisoner.

Thereafter we were virtually in constant contact with the enemy until the time of our disengagement earlier this month. Our job was mainly one of acting as advance mounted scouts for larger forces of British infantry pursuing the retreating Boer forces. As such we were mostly in contact with snipers who had been ordered to act as a rearguard, and they were very deadly at their work. Every day we would ride out and scour the hills for these phantoms, who had the added advantage of blending in with the local inhabitants. Because the countryside was very hilly we had to be careful and were under strict orders from Colonel Steele about "crowning the hills too suddenly." We developed several tricks to avoid this and one of mine seemed to work as well as any. I found an old brolly at an abandoned farmstead and carried it with me. Before topping a hill I would take it out and raise it up and ride along just under the brow. Sometimes a Boer sniper would take the bait and let fly with a volley, giving us an idea of his position before exposing ourselves. Other times we were not so fortunate and a number of my comrades lost their lives in such actions. I was luckier — I had two horses shot out from under me without a scratch to my person!

The boys were pretty headstrong in these activities and some would get out of contact with the main force. Steele would not brook this and would come down pretty hard in his disciplinary measures to keep the ranch boys in line. I even got into a bit of hot water myself on occasion. I had earned my corporal's stripes for my good work at one point, but made the mistake of "borrowing" an officer's cape coat containing some liquor in order to celebrate. Steele learned of this and ordered the coat's return. I complied but it was considerably lightened of its contents, and I was relieved of my stripes and thirty days pay for my troubles. But I was luckier than one poor bloke who got two weeks field punishment for stealing a jar of jam.

Despite being a strict disciplinarian, the Colonel was fair I must admit. While we were with the 3rd Mounted I was ordered to take out a young officer to get him acquainted with the Boers' strategy in the kopjes. We had dismounted and had walked up a hill in order to glass the countryside when this damn idiot stands right up on the knoll just begging a sniper to have a poke at him. I grabbed him by the arm and pulled him back down, calling him a blasted fool. I put my hat on the end of my rifle barrel and held it up so he could see what he would have got if his head had been in it. He was furious and when we returned he complained that I had been discourteous to an officer and should be court-martialed. Steele questioned both of us and after I explained the circumstances he turned to the young officer and gave him a tongue-lashing, saying that I should be thanked for saving his life.

In August we formed the advance guard for Dundonald's column and we were the first troops to enter Amersfoort after routing a Boer unit. After that we overran several Boer trenches and took Ermelo and Carolina. At the end of the month we took part in the attempt to crush General Botha, the main Boer commander, including the Battle of Bergandahl Farm. One of our best days occurred on August 28th when we were in General Buller's attack on Machadorp and I was part of a squadron of Straths that crossed a high hill and took the town in the face of heavy artillery fire. But these Boers were a wily lot and every time we thought we had them cornered they managed to slip away. We spent a whole month pursuing them until we lost them in the mountains in early October and were ordered back to Machadorp.

Everyone thought the war was more or less over at this point and Colonel Steele started making plans for our return home, but as I suspected the Boers were not finished yet. Their best general, de Wet, turned on the column pursuing him inflicting heavy losses and we were soon back out in the field as part of a flying column to relieve General Barton, who was surrounded near Frederickstaad. We broke through de Wet's cordon and took the town, but, as usual, the Boer escaped out onto the veldt and we set out in hot pursuit. Several times we had them pinned down and awaited the infantry for support, but they always moved too slowly and we couldn't hold the enemy.

After a brief respite during which we awaited Colonel Steele's recovery from a dose of ptomaine poisoning (it was the damn bully beef they were constantly feeding us), we again set out after de Wet. It was the same old story as we chased him all over the Orange Free State and the conditions were terrible — wet, cold, short rations and the horses so run down they were a pitiful sight. But not so tired that they couldn't act up as I found to my disgust. One morning while fetching my mount from the remuda in the pre-dawn darkness one of the noted kickers in the bunch caught me off guard and gave me a terrible whack in the leg. It was a bad laceration and I was moved to what passed for a field hospital where some butcher tried to fix me up. The equipment was poor, the surgeon was poor, and the job was poor, and I've been suffering from it ever since.

That put me out of it but I tagged along and helped as best I could. We chased de Wet for five weeks, not pausing long enough to change our underwear as Steele said. The tactics were to drive de Wet up against some fixed fortifications in the north, but he again slipped through. By this time we were nearing the end of our promised one year of service, and I was as anxious to get back to the mountains as many of the boys were to the ranches. Steele brought this to the high command's attention and after some debate about the matter they agreed early in January.

That leads me back to Cape Town today. I will close this entry by stating that this has been a difficult campaign and would have been more successful but for the overcautious attitude of some of the British commanders. I have lost many good comrades in our many skirmishes, but I have also met many others from the Territories whom I shall never forget and shall try to keep in touch with in the future. Strong friendships are forged by what we have gone through together.

* * *

February 14
We had been promised a visit to London on our way home by Lord Strathcona, as many like myself originally hailed from England. Today, after a very leisurely voyage from Cape Town, we put in at the Royal Albert Docks and then marched to Kensington Barracks where we were met by Lord Strathcona, who is High Commissioner for Canada, and several other notable wellwishers. We are to be reviewed by the King tomorrow at Buckingham Palace and everyone is excited and polishing their boots with great vigour. Shortly we are to be given some day leave to visit and I'm greatly looking forward to going out to Welling and seeing everyone again.

February 16
What a glorious day yesterday was — one I shall not soon forget.

In the morning we marched to Buckingham Palace, where on our departure from South Africa we had expected to parade before Queen Victoria, the sovereign under whom we had all lived for so many years and had fought the campaign. But her great reign had ended when she died the day after we embarked, so instead we were presented to the new King, Edward VII. Before a large and boisterous crowd he presented each one of us with the South African War Medal, we being the first troops to receive it. He then presented the regiment with the King's colours, spoke of his late mother's intention to present them personally and called on us to defend them in the future. Colonel Steele was then awarded the Victorian Order, which all the men felt he richly deserved. We then marched past the King back to the barracks, were addressed by Lord Strathcona, posed for photographs and were dismissed for the day.

February 17
This afternoon I took a coach out to Welling to visit the family. It has been more than fifteen years since I have laid eyes on the Old Dover Road that ran through the heart of the village and what changes there have been! This place is now pretty much a part of London and has grown quite a bit. Many of the fields that my father oversaw when I was a boy have disappeared and there are new buildings everywhere. But the familiar landmarks still dominate, in particular the old church which goes back to the time of the Norman Conquest. Walking down the road to the old home I passed

the scene of so much unhappiness in my early life — Foster's Endowed Church of England School — where they tried hard to drill a little history and geography into a rascally lad's head.

On reaching our house I was amazed at how small it looked in comparison to my recollection during the many times my thoughts have drifted back to it on a lonely winter night out on the trapline. I swallowed hard and rapped on the door. It flew open and there standing before me was a lovely girl, my sister Maria who had been born only just before I left. She threw her arms around my neck and kissed me and in the background I heard an unmistakable voice: "That's my Eb, come home to see his old mother."

It was a wonderful visit. Alerted to my coming, most of my brothers and sisters had gathered to see me — Augustus, the eldest, a butcher in Welling, Stephen, a farmer, Henry, a gardener, Sam, a soldier, my sister Ellen, a maid, and my youngest brother Walter, a groom. Another brother, Alfred, an architect, no longer lived close by, but he had written to mother to send his regards. We had many things to talk over and everyone wanted to know about my Rocky Mountain experiences and the war, so the time quickly flew by. Late in the evening I went back to the barracks feeling like I had relived a good part of my life in a very short time.

February 22
The past week has been a continual round of banquets, sightseeing and relaxation for the men of the regiment. On the 17th we attended church and visited with many of the important people of the city, on the 18th all the theatres and

places of entertainment were made available to us and Lord Strathcona held a lunch in our honour, and so it went. I was fortunate in being able to meet briefly with Dr. Collie, who told me about his experiences on the Bush River with Fred Stephens last summer while I was fighting out on the veldt.

I also had another opportunity to go out to Welling and spend a more quiet time with my mother. She asked me if I would consider staying and I went to great pains to explain to her all that Canada and my life in the mountains meant to me and she said that she understood. I told her about this journal, saying that it had originally been intended for her so that she could read about my experiences but that it had now become so much a part of me that I hated to give it up. She told me to keep it and continue it, asking only that I use it to remind me to write her often and relate its contents.

I stayed overnight and was given my old bed to sleep in. I lay there thinking about some of my boyhood escapades but I soon found the mattress far too soft after the places I've been used to sleeping, so I just took the quilt and rolled up on the floor. I awoke early and slipped out without saying goodbye, because she and I both knew it was unlikely that we would see each other on this Earth again. Tomorrow we will take the train for Liverpool and embark on our voyage for Halifax, going home at last!

* * *

March 9
We arrived in port yesterday, six days overdue and feeling wretched after a voyage that made our trip over look like a

picnic. Louis McCallum, who has been with me throughout this episode, took seasick and I did my best to make him comfortable, although at times I didn't feel much better myself. Things brightened up considerably today when we were met by an official of the Bank of Montreal and our paymaster, who informed us that Lord Strathcona had ordered that each of us be given the difference between the pay for the Imperial Cavalry and that of the North West Mounted Police. Since the latter was much higher, the voucher amounted to a tidy sum and will certainly provide me with a bit of a grubstake when I get back to Banff.

We left today by a special train for Montreal and tonight were greeted by a great crowd at Moncton welcoming us home as heroes. Some of the fellows intend to stop over at Montreal for a short while but I will get on the Pacific Express as soon as I can.

March 17
Arrived back in Banff early this morning. I could see the rising sun touching the peaks as we headed west from Calgary and they looked like long lost friends. It seems impossible that I've only been gone for a bit over a year because it feels like many. No one knew I was coming so my arrival was without cheer or fanfare, just the way I wanted it. I've seen enough of that in England and in the east to last a lifetime.

I walked from the station down the river to the shack and went right in, surprising Jack who was sorting some samples. He was full of questions but I just wanted to go out and walk around and take in the snow, sunshine and peaks.

March 30

What a celebration last night — it's taken me all day to clear the cobwebs.

Unbeknownst to Louis and I, the citizens of Banff and Anthracite arranged a little "do" for us to mark our service and our safe return home. It began at the Pavilion with a feast fit for a King at which 150 or so sat down to join us. Following that Mr. Douglas, the Park Superintendent, was the master of ceremonies for a program of speeches and song rendered by some of the villages' notables, including Frank Beattie and Dr. Brett. I was particularly moved by the old Scotsman, David Galletley, who recited a stirring rendition of "Soldiers of the Queen." The official part ended when Ralph Edwards made a presentation to us on behalf of the citizens, both Louis and myself receiving an engraved gold locket recording our service to Queen and Country. We were both called upon to speak, but I was so moved that I can't even recall what I said, although I'm certain it was short and to the point. After that the tables were moved back, a Calgary orchestra was brought in and the music and revelry flowed until the wee small hours.

I'm not much of one for public displays, preferring the pine of the woods to that of the dance floor, but I must admit that it's nice to know how many good friends one really has and how your fellow man appreciates your efforts on his behalf.

XII
1901

May 24
Queen Victoria's birthday today and quite a little gathering amongst us Englishmen to mark her passing this year.

I've been thinking over my future since arriving home — in fact I even chewed on it some during quiet moments in South Africa and England. While I could easily live the life of a prospector and trapper, I don't see that it's too predictable, particularly if I ever want to settle down and have a family. With the extra pay we received from Lord Strathcona and the bit I can borrow around here, I'm thinking of starting on a guiding operation instead.

While I was away fighting the Boer, Tom Wilson began to branch out to Laggan and Field. He rightly sees that the real profit in this line of work is in the long trail, rather than fooling around with day-trippers and hotel guests. The men with the money — the Alpine Club types and the American hunters — all want to get as far away from the railway as possible and setting up at Laggan and Field certainly keeps him in a position to fit the bill. But I know some of these gents pretty well myself now having guided and swapped lies around a campfire with them all at one time or another, and I think if I keep my outfit small and offer my personal services I can attract my fair share.

May 28
Mr. Mathews arrived today to begin opening up the hotel for the season and I told him what I had in mind about

going into business on my own. While he wouldn't promise me anything, having worked with Tom for many years, he did say that if the season shaped up well there should be plenty of work for everyone. He explained that two years ago the company had noticed an increase in traffic as the depression began to loosen its grip, and the CPR put on a second daily transcontinental, the Imperial Limited. He claimed that last year it had brought with it a good growth in the number of guests at the hotel, with all signs showing it would continue this year. I could tell from his manner that he was pleased with my idea and I believe I will be able to depend on him for some parties.

June 8
Lady Luck looks like she's smiling. Today I had a wire from one of my Strathcona compatriots, George Kerr from Moosomin, Saskatchewan, who met the great Edward Whymper on the train from the east.

Whymper is the famous English mountaineer who first climbed the Matterhorn back in the sixties, and there has been much carrying on here about his impending arrival. Mr. Shaughnessy, the head of the CPR, has given him the support of the company to come with his Swiss guides and climb in the Rockies so that he can report on his experiences in newspaper and magazine articles. George, who had stayed to visit in the east after we disembarked in March, was talking with him on the train and when he learned where he was headed he suggested he look me up. Whymper enquired why and when told of my guiding exploits he apparently said I sounded like the type he could use, and George gave him a note of introduction.

June 9

I met Whymper up at the hotel this morning. He looks like a tough old bird, as he is now in his sixties and gives the appearance of having done some hard living. Some say that his experience climbing the Matterhorn, when a rope broke and four of his climbing companions plunged to their deaths, left him aloof and bitter. I've also heard rumours that he sometimes gets in his cups a little too much and that he can be real ornery to deal with, a fact attested to by one of the waiters I know who had served him at breakfast. However, there's nothing I enjoy more than putting a superior Englishman in his place on the trail and given time I'm sure that we can work out a truce.

I had a long confab with him about his plans, which are to explore the Lake Louise and Yoho regions looking to claim some unclimbed peaks with his retinue of four Swiss guides and a photographer. The thought of four Swiss guides made me shudder, but I kept my opinion to myself. He was a hard bargainer and it took awhile to convince him that he would not get Wilson to supply him with men for as good a rate as mine, and we eventually settled on $2.50 a day for my services, $2.00 for a packer and four-bits a horse.

He wants to get away as soon as he's organized and the weather clears up a bit, so I'm to come around and see him tomorrow to receive our marching orders. It looks like I'm in business!

June 13

I've got eight horses down at the shack waiting for this damn abominable weather to clear so that we can get on with the Whymper business. It has become clear we will be unable to start at Lake Louise as early as he had hoped due to the backwardness of the season and he has decided that we will do some exploring in the Vermilion Pass area while we wait. Jack has somewhat reluctantly agreed to pack, but only because the snow in the high country is keeping him from our diggings. We will not be covering a great deal of ground, so the Swiss can walk while we use most of the horses for packing the huge amount of truck that Whymper has brought with him. He told me he shipped thirty-eight boxes from London!

It was still sleeting and snowing today and Whymper came down from the hotel to tell me that we will not leave until things clear up a bit. In the meantime he wants me to show him around the Banff area and help capture some wildlife specimens. This isn't really what I had in mind, but I guess it's work.

June 17
We've spent the last few days traipsing around trying to keep warm in the snow and cold, listening to the Swiss guides grouse about how they're being mistreated. They claim they were hired to climb instead of being porters, but to me they seem a lazy lot that try to make excuses for getting out of work. Whymper's got a temper and feels that he is from a higher station in life than us ordinary folk, so things have been mighty difficult already. It doesn't bode well for the next few months we're supposed to spend together, but I've staked myself on this deal and I'm going to have to bite my tongue.

On Friday Whymper sent the guides, whose names are Klucker, Pollinger, Bossoney and Kaufmann, his photographer Francklyn, and myself out to try gather some specimens of eagles. We succeeded in killing an adult along the river near Vermilion Lakes and after finding the nest captured one of the young ones live. Saturday, which was as miserable a day as I've seen at this time of year, we rented some boats and rowed up the river to one of my best fishing holes, where much to my surprise we caught fifteen trout. We spent the rest of the day playing like we were the English navy (with Swiss deckhands) on the Vermilion Lakes and even though we were wet and cold Wymper insisted we stay out until early evening.

This afternoon he told me that he has finally got the blessing of the CPR higher-ups to stop the train at Castle so he can ride up in comfort. Jack and I will start out early with the horses over the tote road and meet them there. He had prepared an agreement setting out the terms of our earlier discussion and almost against my better judgment I signed it. I'm now committed— or maybe I should be!

June 21
We set up a base camp near the summit of Vermilion Pass five days ago so that Whymper could do some climbing and exploring to determine the source of Hector's descriptions of the mountains in this region. While he sets out ambitious plans for the day's activities, he mostly seems content to stay in camp and direct "the help" as to what to report on rather than doing it himself.

A few days ago while the Swiss were sent off to explore

towards Mount Ball, Jack and I went down the Vermilion Valley to try find a little game, but much to Whymper's chagrin only managed to bring back a few bull trout. He took this as evidence that we had done nothing all day. Later we started cutting a trail over to the Ball Valley and when we got back to camp he asked the Swiss if we had worked hard. Fortunately for their hides they said we had.

June 24

It only stopped raining long enough in the last three days to allow it to snow, and we were all going crazy imprisoned in our camp. Yesterday I couldn't take it anymore and told Whymper in the afternoon that I wanted to go in search of a lake and valley I've heard of which connects with Wilcox's Consolation Valley. I didn't hold much hope of finding it, but it was good to get away by myself for a few hours so I wouldn't be thinking about wringing his neck.

Today he came to the happy conclusion that we were going to run short of supplies and has sent me back to Banff to ask Mathews to supply us with more. I have with me one pack horse to bring back the bacon, beans, potatoes (and scotch) he has requested, and tonight I am camped beside the Bow with the snow falling gently and wetting everything thoroughly. Even the bugs have disappeared in this damn backwards season.

June 27

Returned to camp yesterday afternoon while W. and the others were out climbing the peak named after Francklyn, looking for the elusive Mount Ball. While at Banff I learned the railway had been washed out by floods and there was no traffic running. Mathews was not moved to let too much food go in these circumstances, but he did give me the necessities.

When Whymper returned I gave him a letter from Mathews and told him the news about the line. He seemed unconcerned and told me that yesterday he had discovered the way to Wilcox's long lake. Today I went out to scout the path for horses and think I have it figured out. I caught seven trout in the lake and brought them back to dinner, but found the atmosphere pretty frosty in camp. Jack tells me that Whymper and Klucker had a big blow-up just after I left and that the old man has spent much of the day writing the guides a letter pointing out their many sins. Sounds like things are pretty normal around here.

July 2
We arrived at the chalet at Lake Louise today after a good day's pull through the rain from where we camped at the Eldon siding last night. Whymper finally got disgusted a couple of days ago with the weather and his lack of success in reaching the foot of Mount Ball from the Vermilion Valley and sent Jack and me off to cut trail from the pass down to the Bow. It was rough going considering the weather, but it did keep us out of the old man's way and even today we chose to push on ahead of him in the rain rather than have to listen to him complain as we headed for Lake Louise. I can't say as I blame him in his remarks about the weather though, as here we are at the beginning of July with nary a completely bright and warm day to account for.

Tonight when we reached the chalet and got everything

unpacked Whymper was writing up his own journal and shared his description of the names of the days of the week with me. He's called them Stormday, Rainday, Mistday, Hailday, Thunderday, Snowday and Sleetday. We should be able to keep our powder dry for the next while though as he wants to do some exploring in the region of the lake and I'm to stand by here at the chalet and tote up supplies by horse to whatever camps he decides to establish.

July 20

Our headquarters are now at Mount Stephen House at Field, where we came a few days ago so that Whymper can commence his survey of the Yoho Valley and Emerald Lake area. We are starting with a look at the fossil beds on Mount Stephen, one of the few subjects on which Whymper and I see eye to eye. He had expressed an interest in minerals and fossils and so I told him of these beds, which I first visited myself more than ten years ago. I think this is where I picked up my first sample of Cambrian trilobite and I still believe they contain the best specimens in these mountains. Its hard to fathom that this slope some 2500 feet above the valley was once the floor of a warm ocean where these creatures lived in abundance, but that's what makes this fossil hunting business so fascinating.

Whymper sent us on ahead last night to make sure the trail was clear and this allowed me time to hunt through the shards and pieces to find some complete specimens. W. and the four guides didn't arrive until the middle of the afternoon and after showing him a few good samples that I had left to please him, we were on our way back to the hotel for supper.

July 24
For the past few days Jack and I have been ferrying supplies to the top of the pass above Emerald Lake so that Whymper can commence his assault on the Yoho Valley. On Monday we took eight full loads and as the weather was very hot the horses were exhausted by the time we got to the little tarn on top, so we decided to set up camp at this delightful spot instead of in the thick of the valley as Whymper wanted.

Today when I got back to Field he was very upset with my decision but I informed him that it was best to camp in the open near a good supply of water in the heat. It was hard for him to argue since his thermometer showed the temperature to be over 100 degrees in the sun this morning.

July 26
Made a quick trip from the camp at the pass down to Field today to bring up the last of the supplies. Two of the horses are very down in the dumps and I told Whymper that I may have to take them to Banff or risk losing them. I also told him I wasn't up to snuff myself — I feel like I'm coming down with the same affliction that laid me low on one occasion in South Africa and if so it'll be Hell. He seemed unconcerned and sent me off for the pass again shortly after noon. I'm alright for the moment, so here's hoping.

July 29
I feel like I've been boiling in Satan's own cauldron and am only just beginning to feel human again tonight. The last few days are only a blur, but Jack told me the details, and they are not pretty. He fed me copious amounts of Whymper's supply of quinine and chlorodyne and that got

me through the worst of it.

Despite feeling weak this morning I went out to do my best to help clear the trail. In the afternoon when I came back to camp I went to one of the boxes containing cooking supplies to get something and while doing so Whymper came up and asked in his usual tone what I was doing trying to get into one of <u>his</u> boxes. That was too much given my recent troubles and I lost my temper, giving him a good dose of trail language. When he asked where the Swiss guides were I answered that I had finished clearing the trail myself and that they were probably sleeping somewhere in the bush, as usual. Then the feathers really flew and I decided right there that I had to find some way of getting away before I end up breaking his bloody English neck.

August 2
After a good deal of thought about my situation I told Whymper today that I had to take some sick horses back to Banff. But its really me who needs the break.

I've never met a man who could so irritate me and not even think about or understand how he did so. Yesterday he scolded me for not being quicker to bring the horses to our new camp in the Upper Yoho, paying no attention to my explanation about their state of health. Another violent argument erupted and I became so angry that Jack had to warn me about the way I was carrying on. Things settled down a bit when he agreed to let Jack go to town with the horses, but on reflection I knew it had to be me if I was going to see this contract through. W. got mad again when I informed him, and before I went away I told Jack that I would try find a good man to accompany Whymper on a planned expedition to the Ice River area, once we finish in the Yoho.

One of the Swiss guides, Bossoney, was terribly sick with the same ailment which had afflicted me, so I took him down to the hotel at Field to find medical treatment. Tom Wilson was there and when I told him my tale of woe he agreed to help me out, which I thought was pretty white of him in the circumstances. He said he would make one of his men, Tom Martin, available to Whymper and would check in on the situation himself after he had attended to his business in Field.

August 9
Returned to camp today after a glorious week away from my nemesis. I thought hard about not coming back but being away for a few days made me realize once again how much was at stake. A falling out with Whymper would cook my goose with the CPR, and if we got in a dispute about how much he owed me my ability to pay for the outfit would fast disappear. No, better to get a grip on myself and see it through.

Things had improved quite a bit when I arrived back here. As promised, Tom had joined Whymper a few days after my departure along with the Reverend James Outram. Outram, an English clergyman who has emigrated to Canada, had been climbing with Professor Fay and some friends when the Professor hurt his knee and was unable to continue. Through Tom he was introduced to Whymper, who took an immediate liking to him and invited him to join his camp.

Tom was able to show Whymper a few shortcuts that his previous experience in the Yoho had taught him, and that also put the old man in a good humour.

August 12
Outram and I have been spending the last few days searching for a direct route from the Upper Yoho to the main Yoho Valley at Whymper's direction. This has had its advantages since it has kept me at a distance and allowed my temper to stay cooled. Today we found a route that could be taken by horses, but I think it will take us a few days to chop through it. This evening we returned to Whymper's camp in the Upper Yoho to report on our success, and he told me that tomorrow I am to go to Field to carry some letters he wants posted. While I don't relish being regarded as someone's mailman, it does have the advantage of keeping me out of harm's way.

While spending the last few days with Outram I got to know him quite well. He's ambitious for a man of the cloth and kept asking me about my trip into Assiniboine. There's no doubt that he has an eye to be the first to scale it and as many of the other big peaks as possible. I don't understand what moves him, but such desires could lead to some good business, so I'm feeding him all the information he wants.

August 17
It was too good to last. After a week of peace and tranquility, Whymper and I locked horns again today.

The past few days we have been engaged in moving our camp and equipment up to the Yoho Glacier. I had taken to

travelling ahead of Whymper and the guides to avoid fric-
tion, and had already picked out a campspot near Twin
Falls. My previous trips up the valley had told me that this
was the last decent camp before the toe of the glacier. When
Jack and I reached the spot we found another group lunch-
ing there, comprised of the two Vaux brothers and their sister from Philadelphia and the Swiss guide Hasler. We had a
brief confab with them before setting to work unpacking,
but when Whymper came up shortly afterwards he came
over and commanded that we camp at the end of the glacier and not at the spot that I had picked. I told him in no
uncertain terms he didn't know what he was talking about.
He disagreed and set off toward the glacier to prove me
wrong, soon returning and admitting that I had chosen cor-
rectly. But just to let me know who was boss, he ordered me
to pack up and remove part of the camp an hour back down
the valley to the small warm lake while he and the guides
used this camp to launch an attempt on Mount Collie. I was
seething inside but happily took my leave.

Before clearing out, I had the opportunity to hatch a plan
with Outram. Word had been brought up from Field that a
recent and much heralded attempt by Wilcox on Mount
Assiniboine had failed. Outram had been talking about
Wilcox's plan a few days before and had ruefully expressed
the feeling that if he could only afford to get there he was
certain he could take the peak. By this time I knew that matters had gone too far with Whymper for me to continue on
with him to the Ice River. I therefore proposed to Outram
that I would get him in and out of Assiniboine in record time
and at very little cost if he was prepared to ride hard and
fast. With the news of Wilcox fresh in his mind, he jumped

at the opportunity, and we agreed that as soon as the current work was finished we would make a run for it. Whymper plans to send Outram and one of the guides over a low pass he believes connects with Lower Bow Lake and thence on to Laggan and back to Field by the railway, so it will be a few days yet. I'm already feeling better just thinking about it.

August 22
Yes, I'm now certain I have made the right decision as Whymper has now resorted to writing me letters.

Last night it was decided that Outram, Pollinger and Kaufmann would be sent today to try make it over the pass to Lower Bow Lake as had been previously decided. Whymper wanted to move his camp down near Takakkaw Falls and sent Bossoney to get me, but unbeknownst to him I had moved my camp up from the warm lake closer to him, leaving the horses on the good pasture at the former spot. He was outraged and ordered me to get the horses as quickly as possible so as to complete the move today. I promised to do my best and hurried off on the double quick, returning a few hours later only to find that he had gone off to explore the glacier. It was a case of hurry up and wait, so I decided to go down to my camp and let him come and find me.

My actions occasioned his letter, carried down to me by one of the Swiss, which charged that I had caused him the loss of a day and that if he was not able to get to Field tomorrow he would recover the amount from me. We'll just see about that!

August 24

Thank God! We got into Field today and three months of torture have come to an end.

I arrived here about 10:30 to find that Outram and the others had got off the train a few hours before. Whymper was already waiting for me with fire in his eyes, so I thought it best not to talk to him until I had unloaded everything. I then went over to get paid off and he started going on about my behaviour, my tardiness, my disobedience of his orders and a list of other perceived sins too long to record. I retorted in kind and foolishly said that maybe I would have to take legal proceedings against him. He remarked that if such were to be the case he would pay me nothing until they were over. Here he knew he had me, so I calmed down and he soon did too and made out my account. He owed me $164 for June, $238 for July and $229.50 for August plus another $14.85 for extras. As he had advanced me $28.50 he gave me cheques totalling $617.85.

For a moment I felt like the wealthiest man on earth, but then I remembered how hard earned every dollar had been. Nevertheless, it is going to go a long way toward paying off the outfit once I settle with Jack and with Dave White for the supplies. Tomorrow I will start the packtrain back for Banff and get ready for Outram's arrival. Hallelujah!!

XIII
1901

August 30

I've spent the last few days here at Banff getting everything prepared for our dash to Assiniboine. With a little time to cogitate, I'm worried I painted the picture a mite too bright with respect to how much time and effort its going to take. However, I've made a commitment and now I'm going to have to see it through or lose my reputation.

Yesterday I looked up Wilcox at the hotel and he told me about his attempt on the peak. He described his approach by the south-west side and I picked up a few hints, but I couldn't come right out and ask for advice because Outram wants to keep his attempt a secret. I also had a wire from the latter who told me to expect him and two Swiss guides, Hasler and Bohren, on today's train. I looked over my stock and picked out the six head that have recovered the best and then prepared a camp down by the river near my corrals, as instructed. I met them at the station and, though I felt it was a bit ridiculous, escorted them to the cover of the riverbank and then to their hidden camp. We will leave tomorrow after Jack and I pack the gear they brought with them.

September 1

Only have energy to write a few lines as we have put in a tremendously long day and rain is threatening.

We got away from Banff about noon yesterday and I attempted to get us as close to Simpson Pass as possible so that we could reach the foot of Assiniboine in one long day.

At times I didn't think we would make it, as we met many obstacles of downed timber and steep trails, but after twelve hours without stopping we are at its foot. This is less than half the time it took us to get here on my first trip with Wilcox. Although we are all quite exhausted, we do not have the luxury of resting up and Outram and the guides are to make their first attempt tomorrow. While we are camped at the foot of the steep and forbiding north face, I have recommended to Outram from observation during my visit in '95 that the best chance for success lies on the south-western side. I will accompany them onto the mountain to show them what I think is the best way.

September 3
We've done it! The most elusive and interesting peak in this part of these mountains has fallen and we are celebrating tonight.

We had expected to take two days to reach our goal, but Outram's suggestion that we should make our way around to the south-west face by climbing up above camp and going over a shoulder higher up rather than trying to fight our away around with horses almost brought triumph in one. Only bad weather prevented success yesterday. We gained the south-west side quickly using Outram's suggestion but the visibility was very poor due to thick cloud. Outram invited me to join them on the attempt, but I begged off stating that I would rather do a little prospecting than risk my neck climbing. In truth, I would have given my best horse to accompany them but was worried my inexperience would slow them down and spoil the game. They succeeded in gaining a secondary summit on the ridge but were not able to see the true summit in the poor light until they had descended a good way down. Because of the bad weather we decided to return to the main camp rather than bivouac out, as we had planned, feeling that we now knew a quick route from our main camp. Our return was overtaken by darkness and we had some interesting moments descending the last band of cliffs above camp in the dark.

The sky began to clear last night and the climbers were up and off at ten past six in perfect weather. In about three hours they were back at the point where we had cached our supplies the previous day and began the climb proper. They experienced no difficulty in determining the route they wanted to take, having yesterday's reconnaissance to guide them. The ice built up from the recent wet weather and frosty nights required the cutting of many steps, and they recounted several hair-raising places that had to be detoured. But early in the afternoon they stood on the summit at 11,870 feet above sea level. The summit is apparently a double one, corniced with ice and snow and the view from it as described by Outram is a geographer's dream — he saw peaks as far away as Mount Goodsir and Mount Ball. Emboldened by their success, Outram suggested that they complete a traverse of the peak, descending by the steep north face on their return. His description of this undertaking made me realize that my decision of yesterday not to climb was a good one — I would not have been much use hanging from icy handholds with 2000 feet of nothing below my feet!

As night began to fall we became worried about our comrades, but just before dark we could hear them coming in the distance. Their whoops of joy told the tale and we rushed out to greet them, Jack playing "See the Conquering Heroes Come" on his violin to welcome them home.

September 5

As it turned our victory had been achieved not a moment too soon. When we awoke the next morning it was to a world dressed in white, as it has snowed all night and any mountaineering would have been impossible.

The snow presented me with a bit of a jackpot because now that Outram had carried out his part of the bargain, I had to make good on mine and get everyone back to Banff quickly. The weather was so foul and everything so covered in snow that it took us until past noon to get packed and on our way, and the travelling was no picnic. We traversed what Outram named Desolation Valley and I called a halt at the head of the Simpson Valley, as we were all cold and wet and I knew that one more hard day would get us out.

Today we had to set our course into a driving snow the minute we left camp and it continued to sweep down on us on the heels of a north wind for the entire trek. The soft snow balled up the feet of both horse and man, slowing us to half speed and at some spots in the open the trail was entirely obliterated. But the horses knew where they were going, and in the afternoon we finally hit the Healy Creek stretch and made our way back to the Bow River. The horses could simply not go on so I decided to camp. Outram wanted to get to town so after settling my meagre account he bade Jack and I farewell and with the guides continued on into town. We'll take our time tomorrow morning and savour our success as we return home triumphant!

September 9

Ran into Ike Byers who runs the local newspaper and he
told me he interviewed Outram before he left. He intends to
write an article about the conquest of Assiniboine and I was
able to fill in many of the details. He also convinced me that
if I'm going to take this business seriously I better get my
name out there and so I've agreed to take out an advertise-
ment on a trial basis. It'll read "Bill Peyto, Guide & Outfitter,
Banff, NWT." I've got to admit, it has a nice ring.

XIV
1901-02

November 12
I've sure been getting the accolades around here for the trip to Assiniboine with Reverend Outram. He's got a brother in Calgary who's been telling all and sundry about the first ascent and the job I did in getting him there. If only they knew the half of it. Anyway, this word of mouth stuff can't hurt the new business and Mathews added his congratulations before he left. I'm not that partial to cozying up to the CPR, but it sure won't hurt in getting this outfit on the rails.

I'm going to write brothers Walter and Sam and see if they want to come out and lend a hand. I know when I dropped by the old place on the way home this spring they were at odds and ends, so maybe they'd be interested. Jack's been a good man but I know his heart's set more on gold than this base stuff we've been pulling out of the diggings around here and I don't think he's long for these parts. I'll probably have to find someone else to depend on if things get busy enough next year. Outram said he'd like to come back for a big trip to the north so maybe I can tie into that.

November 15
Talked to a packer today who's got a good reputation around here. His name is Jim Wood and he said he may be interested next year. He had his sister Emily with him visiting from Eburne, B. C. on Vancouver Island. She tells me her father is a merchant there and is the mayor, so the family must be some important. Like Jim, she's got some Indian blood in her and those dark eyes and hair sure make her

mysterious. I think I'll have to get to know her a little better.

November 21
I've been spending some time with Emily lately and we really seem to be hitting it off. It's good that her brother is in the guiding line like me so that she can understand some of the things I've seen and done out there. I haven't run into too many women who could give a tinker's damn about high places, big glaciers and a good feed of sheep around a campfire at night, but she's different. I've got to get back to working on my diggings but I just can't seem to pull myself away right now. We went out for a long trek in the new snow on our snowshoes yesterday and she kept right up to me!

December 1
As I've stated in these ramblings before, I'm not much of one for social dos and dancing, but Emily insisted that I accompany her to a shindig that Doctor Brett put on last night. She taught me a few steps and after stomping on her toes a few times I began to catch on to it. By the end of the evening I was quite enjoying myself — it's downright amazing the things this woman can get me to do!

December 6
Well, I never thought I'd see the day, but this old grizzly has taken the bait good. Today I asked Emily to hitch her star to mine and to my surprise she said yes! I told her that I'll be ornery and harder to handle than a polecat at times and that I'll probably leave her for too long while I'm out in the mountains earning my keep. But she said she doesn't care and that when I'm here I'll make up for it. I hope she's right and I sure as Hell am going to try. We're going to have the

wedding shortly after Christmas and she's already getting excited and has started the planning.

January 7
Emily and I tied the knot yesterday at the home of Dave and Annie White with all our friends in attendance. Jim stood up for me and Emily's cousin from Armstrong, B. C. for her. It's been a long time since I've been dressed up so fancy and it felt kind of strange, but Emily looked like an angel so I had to do my part. We had a small dinner and reception for our friends and the liquor flowed pretty good too. I tried not to get carried away as I wanted to make it a night to remember for both of us, and I think we succeeded. We're going to move into the shack for the time being until we can build something of our own and Jack's kindly agreed to find other lodgings for awhile. I'll take a few days to celebrate and get things straightened away but I'll soon have to get back out on the trapline to try support us. I can go for a couple of days on a hardtack biscuit when the pickings get thin, but I'm sure Emily will expect to eat regular!

* * *

March 1
Had to leave things to tend themselves on the line for a few days as my mind has been pestered about how Emily's doing and worrying about the business next year. I snow-shoed to town in record time and found her in good spirits. She's already been adopted by our neighbour Mrs. White and some of the other local ladies so has lots of company.

There was a letter awaiting me from Mr. Mathews, who I'd written after our wedding. I asked him to speak on my behalf with the CPR brass to see about taking over Tom's place as their guide at Banff now that he seems more interested in Laggan. He stated that while there would be no official authorization to that effect, he saw no difficulty in us working out something for next season. That's all I wanted to hear because I was worried that John Brewster's young boys, Bill and Jim, would be angling for that post. I've heard that the CPR intends to have them represent the company at the Sportsmen's Show in New York this spring, even though they're mere lads and I have more knowledge of these mountains in my little finger than they do in their two heads. Anyway, I'll have to start laying in a few more head at the Montreal Valley place to get ready for the season.

March 3
I started work on the new house today — finally Emily and I are going to have a home of our own. Jack was kind enough to let Emily use his shack for the last while, but we can't stay on there forever. Luckily no one had taken up the lease on that piece where I have my pack shack and which I often use as corral space, so I approached the superintendent about acquiring it. The lease says its Lot 9, Block A and it has all we need for our home and the business, as well as being close to the river and on the edge of town. While I may be a married man now, I still don't want to get too close to this town living. It won't be much of a place to begin with — it'll be about ten by fourteen feet — but I'll do the best log work I can and together we'll build it up. Emily's fine hand is sure to make it comfortable.

March 5
Received a letter from Victoria today from the Reverend. He

confirmed the plans he mentioned to me before leaving last fall. He too has received a lot of good words about our accomplishment and because of it has apparently been able to put together some funds for a big trip to the north. He intimated that some of them may be coming from the CPR, and this may partly account for the tone of Mathews' letter. As there will be three of them and a Swiss guide, I'll need a couple of hands to help me. Although I'm expecting brothers Walter and Sam soon, I don't think I can count on them to go out on the long trail before they get used to the country and the conditions. Emily's brother Jim is willing to work with me and Jim Simpson has expressed some interest as well.

March 9
I've got this place far enough along now so that Emily can move in and start to get things sorted out while I head back out on the trapline. It's getting on towards bear season and if I want to get a grizzly or two this year I better get at it.

The government legislation enlarging the park boundary looks sure to pass now and I'm worried it might wreak havoc with some of our claims. There's still lots of mining and prospecting going on around here but they're talking about tightening up on the hunting and fishing regulations and God knows what will be next. Jack's been getting mighty itchy since I took up with Emily and has been talking lately of giving it up here and heading out for the real gold in South Africa He's going to leave Dave White in charge of his place in case he decides to come back. He and I have been through a lot together and I don't think I have a better friend in this world, so I'm going to miss him. He told me that if he doesn't return all the claims are mine, and he gave me a written statement to that effect. I hope he changes his mind and that his shadow will fill my door again before too long.

*   *   *

June 16
Its been a busy couple of weeks, but I think I've finally got things straightened away to put this outfit to the test this summer.

Mr. Mathews told me after his arrival that he would like to see a regular pony stand set up for his guests that would give them a good day's outing along with some views of the mountains. We discussed the possibilities and I suggested that the new government trail to the top of Sulphur Mountain might fit the bill. The view out over the town to Lake Minnewanka is a fine one and with a bit of work Walter and Sam should be able to handle this mostly by themselves, so we'll start on it in a few days.

Yesterday I sent Jim Simpson and Fred Ballard out to clear the trail near Bear Creek in preparation for Outram's party. As time allows, they will continue on up the north fork so we won't be delayed too much in getting to the big peaks he wants to climb.

June 20
Received a wire from Outram today telling me that plans have changed because the two dudes he intended bringing along have dropped out. That means there will only be him

and the Swiss guide Kaufmann unless he can recruit some replacements in a hurry. That might not be too bad though, because the way things are shaping up around here we're going to need all the horseflesh we can get just to handle the local business. With only thirty head to go around, I'll have to make the most of every one of them.

I had intended on accompanying the Reverend's party myself for at least the first few weeks but I may leave it up to Jim and Fred now. Jim's learned enough to be a good guide and is pretty familiar with that country and Fred, who used to work for Tom as well, is one of the better trail cooks around. I think it best for me to stick around here and make sure the hotel is happy with our agreement while we iron out any kinks.

June 26
Outram arrived yesterday and wants to begin about the first of the month for the north. He hopes to link up at some point with a group of Englishmen led by Dr. Collie who have their eye on Mount Forbes and the scalps of some of the other big ones that he covets himself. Fred Stephens is outfitting Collie's gang so we'll probably combine our pack-trains and share the work for the first part of the trip north of Laggan.

The weather's been abominably wet for the last few days as is so often the case at this time of the year. Its kind of put a damper on our preparations for the big push of CPR guests that will begin appearing in a few days, but it has given me a bit more time to show my brothers the ropes. Brother-in-law Jim is going to help out here at Banff while I assist in packing in the victuals we're going to cache for Outram at the Saskatchewan and make sure that Jim and Fred know what I expect of them.

July 2
We've had to postpone our departure for the Saskatchewan because of the foul weather, and yesterday Outram and Kaufmann left for a few days at the Lake Louise Chalet to limber up their climbing skills while they wait. I'm chomping at the bit to get this thing underway so I can get back here and make sure everything goes according to plan. Yesterday was our first day at the pony stand, but there were very few takers in the rain. Today was a bit better and we took five up to the top of Sulphur. The trail was a bit greasy and slippery in places but Walter did fine in the lead. I'm going to spend the next few days fixing up the worst spots so we don't have any accidents — I don't want anything to derail this business with the hotel after I've staked so much on it.

* * *

July 9
Jim, Fred and I arrived at Laggan this morning after bringing the packtrain over on the tote road from Banff. We've got fourteen head and Molly's two-year old colt, which won't be able to be used just yet. Ten will be used for packing the grub to our proposed cache and then I'll bring a few of them back. I don't want my first long trail outfit to run short of anything so I've laid in extra canned milk, tongue, birds and beef, oatmeal, dried fruits, soups and coffee and tea.

It appears I was wise to bring lots of animals and my biggest pack boxes as Outram's kit is something to behold. He's got cameras and plates, a transit and tripod and various other survey and climbing gear, books, notebooks and maps and just about everything else one could find in an outdoors store. The boys were particularly boisterous in their comments when he showed us the latest in camping comfort — an air-mattress made of India rubber complete with a small accordian pump to fill it. We opined that things were sure going to Hell when we were expected to sleep with the strange smell of some rubber brought half way around the world in our nostrils when there's fragrant pine boughs available all around us. But he's paying the bills and I guess he can sleep on rubber or whatever else suits him.

July 11
We've joined up with Fred Stephens' bunch of fifteen that are headed out to cache supplies in the same general vicinity as us. His dudes won't be following for a few weeks yet, so the Reverend will get the jump on them.

Outram has been ranging ahead and behind our cavalcade to get photographs and do some survey work, which is a good thing as I'm sure our language in getting some of these rank new knotheads whipped into shape would not be appealing. I've given him Nigger to ride, but I might have to change because he doesn't like being away from the others. Yesterday he broke his halter-shank and the Reverend had to hot foot it to catch him before he really got going and today he uprooted a whole spruce tree and was trotting off with it dangling from the rope when Christian Kaufmann ran him to ground.

The going was rough at first because of the wet ground from the late spring and recent snow. This section of the trail is always mean but right now its nothing but a sea of mud. As we moved along I could hear the sucking sound as the horses took each step and they were constantly straying from the path as they tried to find better footing, causing us no end of extra work. Kootenay got his pack stuck between two spruces with his hind-quarters in a deep sinkhole and it took five of us pushing and pulling for half-an-hour to get him free. Thank the Lord the weather's improved and we've left the worst behind.

Tonight we're camped at a beautfiful spot on the north end of Upper Bow Lake just in the timber to the west of the inlet creek. Around the fire tonight Jim said that for his money this campsite was the closest one could get to Heaven on Earth and I reckon he's not far wrong.

July 13
Today we put in seven long hours as we made our way down Bear Creek to the Saskatchewan. The views were good at the beginning around Waterfowl Lakes but the last five hours were through heavy timber and we had to get busy with the axes on several occasions despite the fact that Jim and Fred had just recently cleared some three hundred trees from last winter's blowdowns.

The canyon of Bear Creek is always treacherous and this time was no exception. When we got to the mouth we had to ford and, as usual, the water was very swift and was rolling boulders along the bottom causing me some concern. We cached our supplies at the trapping cabin near the mouth and then I decided to help Jim get the outfit to the north side before taking my leave.

Shortly afterwards, while fording the middle fork at the same point as I had taken Collie's party over in '98, we ran into some real trouble. I sent Jim across in the lead and at first the horses followed fine, but when the water got deep they balked and turned back despite Fred's and my best efforts to head them. I then decided to lead with Pet and for the first time in her life she let me down. We were about half way across when the current spooked her and she ducked me off. I grabbed onto the horn and tried to keep on the downstream side while gently coaxing her back to the near shore. We made it back fine and I decided that we would have to take the cayuses across a few at a time. Jim came back over to help and that did the trick. I turned things over to Jim wishing him good luck and they were soon on their way headed for the ford of the north fork while I turned back to cross the middle fork.

Tonight I'm camped at the trapping cabin with the three animals I'm taking back and we'll push hard so that we make Banff in three days. This business sure is going to keep me on the move.

XV
1903

July 15

Jim Wood set off today with ten horses to meet the big German party we're taking to the headwaters of the Athabasca this summer. He'll rendezvous with them and one of the Swiss guides at Laggan and head north. I'll join him when things settle down here a bit. We're getting lots of sightseers from the hotel now and Walter and Sam have been kept going real steady. It isn't very exciting but it sure helps to pay the freight.

I've got the Longstaff family from England booked in a few weeks and although they don't intend on going far afield I plan to guide them myself. They specifically requested my personal attendance on the recommendation of Mr. Stutfield, whom they know well. They'll be bringing along their six children, so it will be quite a group. Emily's been feeling poorly again lately and I'll ask if they don't mind if I take her along. I think she would enjoy getting out and being with some young folk.

July 23

Emily and I are at the Bookrest now getting things ready for the visit of the Longstaffs. They informed me in a letter a few days ago they would like to take a few excursions into areas that are off the beaten track but not too difficult for some of the younger children. I immediately thought of this spot, even though I don't make a habit of bringing people up here.

It's been real fine for us to spend a little time at this lovely place together. Emily's delicate health doesn't allow her to visit during the cold of winter and I was just too busy to take time out to show her around last summer. She says she loves the beautiful larches and wonderful flowers that do so well in these alpine uplands and particularly enjoys the view over the little lake towards the ridge to the southwest. She says she's shocked at the condition of my cabin but I tried to explain the type of life I lead here and distract her with some of my ore samples and the little homes I've made for my animal guests. We never really had a honeymoon after our wedding and these past few days have been as close as we're likely to come.

July 29

Emily and I returned to Banff tonight after camping with the Longstaff family at the amphitheatre on the backside of Cascade. We went out there for a relaxing few days, and the exceptional weather and the pleasure of the company have made it a wonderful outing. I'm not used to such a leisurely existence in the middle of the summer and the fact that I'm able to spend it with Emily makes it all the more satisfying. When we got back from the Bookrest a few days ago she went to see Doc Brett and came home with the wonderful news that we're going to have a baby! I can't ever remember being as happy as I am right now, and if I wasn't so worried about her health things would be perfect.

Today a couple of the young ladies and gentlemen accompanied Mr. Longstaff and myself on a climb of Cascade. It wasn't difficult, although we had to watch out for the girls. He had made arrangements with a friend of his at the hotel to heliograph a message from the summit at a certain time and, as the sun was shining brightly all day, it worked wonderfully.

August 5

Returned today from another little outing with several of the Longstaffs to my place at Simpson Pass as we had planned. Mr. Longstaff and four of the children — Tom, Gilbert, Beatrice and Katherine — accompanied me and we camped, explored the meadows and did some fishing for a couple of days. The young folk were quite taken with the mine and all the tools and implements I use in it, but they were even more excited to try catch the few ground squirrels and voles that frequent the place. We managed to tame down the whiskey jacks that are my regular visitors and before we left they were eating out of our hands. The time with this delightful young family has made me look forward more than ever to when Emily will have one of our own — it won't be long now.

Tomorrow we're joining up with the rest of the family for an overnight trip up the Spray Valley for a little fishing at a spot I know there. Then its back to Banff and the Longstaffs will be off for Victoria and I'll head out on the double quick to find Jim and the Germans on the Athabasca.

XVI
1904

February 13
Emily and I lost our baby a few days ago — it was stillborn.
I had been worried about how things would go because of
her health ever since we learned of her pregnancy last summer. After Christmas I began to have a feeling of foreboding
about it, although I kept it to myself. I talked to young
Doctor Brett and he agreed there could be some problems,
so all in all I was prepared for the worst. Poor Emily is still
in the hospital and is so downcast I don't know whether I'll
ever see that beautiful smile again. I've been doing my best
to try cheer her up and told her we would try again, but I
have my doubts about our chances after this.

February 24
This has been a damnable month and by the sound of things
its going to get worse.

Today I heard a rumour that the hotel authorities of the CPR
have decided that they want contracted outfitting and guiding services next summer and that they are going to offer
them to the Brewsters. I can't figure where I've gone wrong
because I've done everything they've asked of me over the
past two seasons and sometimes I've paid a price for it. It
must be a political fix because I know that John Brewster has
been cozy with the Liberals ever since he helped A. L. Sifton
get elected in this district and there's no doubt the railway
higher-ups are likewise inclined. I've never played that
game, in fact I've never bowed to any man and have damn
little use for anyone who does. Why does life always deal

what's clean and good in this world such cruel blows?

March 4
I learned a little bit more about this Brewster deal when I was down in Calgary talking to some of the local CPR men yesterday. Apparently Bill and Jim are going into partnership with those two college boys they had out with them the last couple of years, Phil Moore and Fred Hussey. Like so many of their type, they have more money than they know what to do with and so are going to invest it in a new company they will form with the Brewsters. They'll need every cent they can lay their hands on because with partners like those boys there will be no end of places to spend it.

I tried to plead my case and was told that these decisions are made at a much higher level than the Calgary office. I said I would write to Mathews about it, but apparently Mr. McLaren Brown, the superintendent in charge, now makes all these decisions himself. Its a good thing I've already made arrangements with a few parties for next season because if this thing goes like it looks it might the pickings could get mighty thin.

* * *

July 1
Today's Dominion Day and normally I would be getting ready for all the hotel dudes that turn up around here at this time thinking they can ride a horse. But that's all gone now with the new order of things in this place. Those confounded Brewster boys are welcome to it, because I never made any real money at it anyhow.

I had a long talk with Walter and Sam a few days ago about where this outfit's going. I told them I'd give them what work I could but that I need men with a bit more trail experience for the type of clients I've got lined up this year. Walter said that he'd been offered a job by Doc Brett as a teamster and that he thought he would take him up on it. Sam is a pretty good blacksmith, and he said he figured he could catch on somewhere.

In a few days I'll be taking Mr. Francklyn, Whymper's old photographer, on the start of a one-month outing to some of our beauty spots so that he can take some plates for a publication he's doing. While I don't relish anything that reminds me of that old s.o.b. Whymper, I never did have any trouble with Francklyn and I have to take my business where I can get it. We'll start out at Lake Minnewanka and then Jim Wood will take him on to Louise and Assiniboine.

July 27
Jim returned today from Mount Assiniboine with Mr. Francklyn in tow and both reported on what a fine time they had. Francklyn said he got some views of the peak that he feels will rival Wilcox's in their quality. If he's achieved that it will be some doing because from what I've seen of those plates, which I packed so carefully through all kinds of country, they're just about the finest ever taken. Francklyn says the Department of the Interior, which is responsible for this park, is interested in purchasing some of his views to illustrate their reports and publications, so they should get good exposure.

Tomorrow we'll get everything straightened out and give

the ponies a few days rest before they head back to the same spot. Our next client is Gertrude Benham, an English lady climber with a big reputation, who plans to be the first one with skirts to the top of old Assiniboine. She heard of my exploits around there from Outram and knows that we are the most experienced and successful outfit for that region. As she plans to take the Kaufmann brothers as guides for the climb, we'll need about seven horses. I've decided to send out Jesse Trot, a new man with a good reputation, to cook and help Jim.

With Emily pregnant again I'm going to keep myself busy as close to home as possible.

August 1
Miss Benham and her Swiss guides came down to Banff from Laggan on No. 96 this morning and I met them at the station. I took them over to the house to wait while the final packing was being done and over a cup of tea had some time to find out a bit about her. She's an interesting study for a woman because to hear her exploits one would assume they were those of a man. She tells me she's already climbed over 100 peaks including the Matterhorn and Mont Blanc and that she bagged a few more good ones around Lake Louise lately. She's also apparently very tough, for she described a recent outing where she and a guide left Lake Louise at midnight and went over the pass into Lake O'Hara, around it and down the Cataract Valley and then up a shoulder of Mount Stephen to its summit and finally down to Mount Stephen House at 3 a.m. the next morning. Things are sure changing in this old world and I expect that we'll see more of her kind out here every year from now on.

August 8

The Benham party returned from Assiniboine yesterday with the welcome news that she had succeeded in her quest with apparent ease. Jim told me she was as tough as I had thought, because she walked rather than rode most of the way and had experienced no difficulty in conquering a peak that has defeated so many. She told me that our services had been excellent in every way and that I could use her for a reference if I wished. It sure won't hurt me to be able to advertise that I've outifitted two out of the three parties to succeed on Assiniboine, and one of them a woman at that!

* * *

November 20

Hallelujah! The Good Lord has finally seen fit to smile on Emily and me — we have a healthy baby born yesterday and its a boy! I was so worried things would go wrong after the last time and she did have a pretty rough go with the birth, but she's feeling in the pink now. We've decided to name him Robert William Fitzgerald Peyto, but I've already taken to calling him Robin. He's going to be one Hell of a man for these mountains once he gets a bit older because I plan to teach him everything I know. I can't wait to get at it!

XVII
1905

July 4

Wilcox finally got generous and gave me a copy of Camping in the Canadian Rockies yesterday. He autographed it "To my friend Bill Peyto" but if he really meant it he sure could have been quicker about it since its been out about eight or nine years now. I guess I did have a brief look at it when it first appeared because I remember how good the plates looked after I had expressed some doubts the first time I had to pack that camera of his. Looking back in this journal I see I also managed to get a few of them wet, but it didn't seem to do any harm.

July 5

I stayed up real late last night reading "Camping" from cover to cover. I hadn't realized before how much of a character Wilcox made me out to be. I guess some of my habits might have appeared a bit odd to a dude used to the refinements of the east but I sure didn't care. He was pretty fair in his comments about my horsemanship and marksmanship, although I think he made me sound more like one of those Yankee cowboys than I prefer. That shot of me on old Chiniquay ain't too bad either and reading about that circuit of Assiniboine reminded me how well he stood up to the country for a business type. A lot of water has gone down the river since then and it put me in mind of how simple and enjoyable life seemed at the time.

Emily continues to be weak and suffer bad health and I know that it's difficult for her to care for young Robin. If I wasn't in a line of work that kept me away from town so much I could help out more, but right now we've got to depend on the good will of some of our neighbour ladies. I'm headed off for a little outing with Wilcox in a few days, so I guess I better get to making the arrangements for her care while I'm gone.

* * *

October 23
Just got off the train from a flying trip down to Calgary to officially enter my homestead in the Montreal Valley. With all the folks starting to move into that country and register their claims, I thought it best to take some action to protect my interests. I entered on the S. W. 1/4, Section 30, Township 27, Range 5, West of the 5th, as that's where my shack and improvements are located. I noticed in the register that no-one has yet filed on two of the adjacent quarters, so I'll tell Walter and Sam to get busy and pick up one each before someone beats them to it.

* * *

November 12
Jim and I have arrived back in Banff from a big sheep hunt that was just about the most successful we've ever had. We took some New York dudes up as far as Wilcox Pass where they got a couple of good rams and then we went over into the Brazeau country that I first eyeballed back in '98 when I was out with Collie and company. We figured that the Indians had been there before us because there was lots of sign of their camps, each with piles of sheep bones in evi-

dence. Something has got to be done about those buggers or there won't be enough game left for an honest hunting guide to make a decent living. Nonetheless, with some good scouting we did find a flock near Brazeau Lake that had some real big fellows and one of our party managed to get a nice head with a 45 inch curl. I also found some of the best arrow points and club heads from prehistoric times that I've seen anywhere in the mountains, and they'll make a nice addition to my collection.

When I got back to town I found Emily and Robin doing well, as Mrs. White has been keeping a close eye on them. The boy's growing so quick now that when I come back from being away for a month I hardly recognize him. He's sure a dandy and I'm going to have to try spend a little time with him now so that he knows who is father is.

November 19
It was Robin's first birthday today and we sure did have ourselves a time. There's been a photographer in town the last few days representing the Sentinel Review Press drumming up business for calendars, and I decided to celebrate the occasion by having him take a picture of Robin to use on an advertising calendar for the outfit next year. He took a shot of me as well but it'll be the boy who gets top billing. With the luck I've had with ladies' parties these past few years I'm going to mention that I make a specialty of them and I'm also going to use the passage from Wilcox's book where he said "Peyto is one of the most conscientious and experienced men with horses I have ever known." It should be the most unusual calendar that anyone in these parts has seen and I hope it attracts some new business.

XVIII
1906

March 6

I had a letter from my brother Stephen today informing me that he's finally going to give Alberta a shake. Both Walter and I have been writing to convince him to give up trying to beat a dead horse being a gardener in the Old Country and get a fresh start here. I guess he also talked with Sam when he got back home last month and got the straight goods. He's got a wife, Maria, and four kids, Annie, Steve jr., Charlie and Lily, and so it's not a decision to be taken lightly. They'll be setting sail in about a week so we'll expect them to arrive next month. I don't have enough work for him, but Walter figures Doc Brett can use another hand at the Sanitarium and doesn't think a man with his experience will have any trouble getting a good position.

April 10

Emily, Robin and I dressed in our Sunday best were accompanied by Walter to the station last evening to welcome brother Stephen and his family to Banff. We got real excited as the train pulled in and waited patiently for them to get off, but they never appeared. We couldn't cotton to what had happened as we had received a wire only a few days ago sending us their travel information. I finally chased down a conductor and asked if a family matching their description had been onboard. "Oh, he said, that must be the family of the lady who made the mistake of getting off at Cochrane." I asked him what he meant by "mistake" and he informed me that the whole of Cochrane was under quarantine for smallpox and that Maria had unwittingly stepped off the train. The authorities refused to let her back on and Stephen and the four children had no choice but to get off and join her.

Walter and I went into the station to try get more information and were handed a wire by Billy Froste, the stationmaster. In it Stephen told us that they were at the hotel and were alright for the moment. We all turned around and went home much disappointed.

April 20
I received a letter addressed to Walter and me from Stephen today reporting that they were all well and liked Cochrane so much they had decided to stay. He's landed a job as a sectionman on the CPR and thinks there is some good opportunity for advancement. If he'd asked my opinion I'd have told him what I think of that outfit, but he didn't and it's his life anyway. I informed Walter and we agreed to go down for a visit to the ranch and then on to Cochrane as soon as the smallpox situation eases.

XIX
1906-07

September 7
This is the most difficult entry I've ever had to write in this journal, but it must be done.

Dear Emily has been taken from us and my heart is broken. Yesterday after dinner I was sitting in front of the fire reading one of my geology books and Robin was fussing in his bed. Emily hadn't been feeling well all week and when she bent down to pick him up and comfort him she was struck by an attack. I got her into bed and ran over to the Whites to get Annie to look after her while I went for Doctor Brett. By the time I got back with him, she was gone — he later told me she'd had a brain hemorrhage. Mrs. White took Robin back to her house and is keeping care of him while I try to pull myself together to do something. Everyone around here has been very kind and asking if they can help, but I just need to be alone right now.

September 10
Well, we laid Emily to rest today in my plot at the Banff Cemetery. The funeral was held at the Anglican Church and it seemed like the whole town was there. She was so well loved by everybody. Dave and Annie White held a small tea in their home afterward which was very kind, but it was almost too much for me. I kept recalling the wedding party we held at the same spot only a few years ago and how happy we had been then.

I've been thinking the past few days about doing a special

stone for her that I can carve myself. There's some good talc up on the headwaters of Redearth Creek and I can picture in my mind a beautiful piece that will provide the kind of memorial she deserves. It's all I can think of right now, but I know I've soon got to turn my mind to more practical things. All I have left of her is young Robin and he's what I have to consider now.

September 21
I can't believe it's already been two weeks since Emily left us. I'm supposed to take out my first hunting party of the fall shortly, but my mind just won't focus on it and so I've asked Jim Simpson to stand in for me.

I've been thinking seriously about the future for the last few days and I've made some decisions. Although it's going to be one of the hardest things I'll ever do, I'm going to have to let Robin go. He needs a woman's hand to raise him and care for him properly and I'm in no position to provide one. I've written to Emily's cousin in Armstrong, B.C., who was always very close to her, and asked if she would care for him. I've just received a letter saying she would.

September 25
Today I write with a heavy heart as I've had to let my own flesh and blood go and I don't know when I'll see him again. Annie White, bless her heart, insisted that she take Robin to Miss McCleary's in Armstrong and as we headed down to the station he was bundled up against the early fall cold. His face looked like an angel's and reminded me so much of his mother that I had to turn away so that I didn't shed any tears. I told him I would come and visit before long but, of

course, he didn't understand and just waved and smiled at me as Mrs. White carried him into the coach. I've seen many a train off at the station but none that marked the end of such a happy time in my life as this one. I know I'll never see such times again.

Tonight I'm packing up as much as I can carry in preparation for heading out to the Bookrest tomorrow. Billy Warren has a few of my cayuses out on a trip to the Saskatchewan with Mrs. Schäffer from Philadelphia and Jim will take care of the rest of the stock here while I'm gone. I'll come back down in a few weeks to pack in my winter supplies to the mine and then take the whole bunch down to the ranch. Then it'll be back to the Bookrest for the winter and perhaps more. I think it'll be a damn long time before I want to see or talk to anyone again.

* * *

June 15
I'm now out at the ranch getting the packstring ready to trail into Banff in the morning. It's later than usual but with the winter we've just been through, which all the old timers agree is the worst in memory, the last of the snow is just disappearing and the trail dried up enough to get them through. The ponies are a little thin and I'll have to fatten them up a bit at Banff before we can take on any hard going.

Over this bastard of a winter when I had to spend so much time holed up, I thought hard about giving up this outfit altogether. The solitary life of the trapper and prospector has even more appeal to me now since Emily's passing and

Robin's leaving. But I've put too much sweat and hard cash into it to just give it away and I'll have to see what the season brings before making up my mind for good.

Looking over the pages of this journal reminds me of all the interesting country I've travelled, dudes I've met and experiences I've had. But those days seem to be gone forever with so many parties on our old trails now, the game all shot to Hell and so much of the country to the north in the hands of timber interests. I reckon there's still a few peaks, valleys and lakes somewhere that are untouched, but all the good clients now seem to be going to the Brewsters and my old friends like Jim Simpson and Bill Warren. I guess I never was one to have a sunny disposition if there was a burr under my saddle, nor did I have the patience and business sense that this line of work requires. No, I'll have to be content with the little bit I can rustle up in Banff this summer as I haven't got anything booked. Perhaps with all the attention to coal prospecting going on the last few years I can look to some customers from that direction.

* * *

October 1
It's been a poor season in every sense of the word, and I've decided to give up on this occupation. My heart's just not in it anymore.

Billy Warren has offered to buy most of the bunch and after a bit of haggling we've agreed on a price. He's familiar with some of them as he used a few on his trip with Mrs. Schäffer last year. He'll need them for a big expedition they're planning next year to an unknown lake north of the Brazeau one of the Stonys told them about. I've always prided myself on my stock and he's going to get some good horses in the deal. There'll be eleven in all and many of them are old friends, especially Wilcox, who was with me the first time I went to the pass that he's named for, and Bessie, who is always full of fire. The others are Frank, Buck, Splash, Silver Peter, Pinky, Midget and the Twins, Lucy and Biddy. Billy is also willing to take all my tack, so I'll not do too badly on the deal.

October 10
After selling off the outfit I figured there was no sense hanging on to the house, shed and corrals. I won't need all the property to care for when I don't intend to spend any time in town and besides the place just makes me melancholy when I think of Emily and Robin everytime I'm alone. I've found a vacant lot out on the Banff Road and I'll build a little shack there that'll take care of my town needs. David McDougall from Morley has offered to buy this place and I figure I'll accept and cut all my old ties.

XX
1909-10

August 3

I found this journal today when I was going through some old papers I'd thrown in the corner of the house right after I tacked it together. I'd almost forgotten that I'd ever kept it in the haze of heartache and whiskey that followed my selling off the outfit and the old place after Emily's death. Leafing through it brought back some good memories with the bad, and I've decided to take it up again, at least for the moment.

Having stopped recording my life for so long, about all I can say is I've managed to survive. Most of my time has been spent in my usual round of hunting and trapping and at the Bookrest trying to see if I can make a going proposition of the copper. I haven't given up on it yet, but most of the shafts I've sunk show good colour for a few feet and then peter out, leading me to speculate if there's a true vein or only small pockets. That and the difficulty of getting a tote road up there to haul out any ore in paying quantities gives me some doubt, but I'm not through trying just yet.

I haven't been too cozy with many folks lately, preferring the company of Lightning to the human kind. He's a tough little terrier and together we've discovered some spots in these mountains that no one else even thought existed. One exception is Norman Sanson, the museum curator and weather recorder, who has so many interests similar to mine that we're naturally curious about what each other is up to. He arrived here about the same time as me, attracted by the wildlife, geology and flora, and since taking over responsibility for the museum about ten or twelve years ago has put together an amazing collection. We occasionally chew the fat about our fossil and Indian finds and of late have started going out on the odd little collecting expedition around Minnewanka and other spots off the beaten track. Norman's a bit of a loner like me and pretty competent in these mountains in his own right, so I have a lot of respect for him. That's more than I can say for most of the inhabitants of this damn burg — they would get lost the minute they're off one of the confounded buggy roads they've taken to building all over the place.

August 20

As hard as it will be to look myself in the mirror, I've agreed to do a little guiding for the Brewster outfit this season.

Jim Brewster has turned out to be a good man in the mountains, even though he was a little too big for his britches when he was a youngster. For a couple of years he lived at the coast while his brother Bill ran the show here, but he did keep up his interest in some timber licenses he and Fred Hussey have over on the Simpson River. This year he's taken over the running of all the Brewster interests and realizes he's got some problems with the reputation of the outfitting end. I suppose that may be why he asked me to sign on for a few trips, since I never had that problem in my heyday. A lot of sand has gone through the hourglass since he and Bill beat me out of the CPR concession, but I blame that more on the railroad than them anyway. One thing's for sure, it'll be nice to have some real change in my pockets no matter what people think of me.

August 27
Arrived back in town today after a four day outing guiding my first party for the Brewster company. It consisted of a very nice American gent named Colgate and his teenaged son, who I took fishing at Sawback Lake. I had one helper for the six head of horses we took and overall it was a very pleasant few days. But this business has sure gone to pot in the past ten years with so many parties in the field. We were only one of three separate groups that Brewster had going to Sawback Lake at that time and the trail up Forty-Mile Creek was like Banff Road. When we got to the lake there was so many dudes fishing there that we almost had to stand in line for a good spot.

I hadn't been at the lake for some years and was disgusted at the number of campsites and the tins and broken glass littering the ground of what had been a beautiful little meadow on my last visit. They're sure as Hell going to ruin this country right smartly if they allow so many people to spread all over the place and run amok like this!

* * *

October 16
I had a little confab with Norman Sanson last night and he offered me an interesting proposition. It seems the government is interested in increasing the population of the new zoo he's building in the park next to the museum and is willing to pay a good dollar for healthy specimens. They're most interested in lynx and wolverine, although Norman said that they could be convinced to take a couple of bear cubs as well. Live trapping any of the above is a tall order,

but if there is anyone in these parts who knows their ways and can outsmart them its me. The $25 a head they're willing to pay would come in mighty handy right now.

October 25
It didn't take me long to make good on Norman's offer.

I've been keeping my eye on a family of lynx up Sunshine Creek and decided to try pick up on one. I stayed at a little cabin I have up against a rock wall near the junction of Sunshine and Healy Creeks and built a couple of deadfall snares baited with a young deer that happened by. I kept clear for a few days so as not to taint the setup with my scent and a couple of days ago was successful in snaring a young male by the right front foot. Now I had the bull by the horns and had to do something with him.

I began by putting on my gloves and gauntlets and then doused a rag attached to a short pole with chloroform. I had also cut a longer pole that I could use to hold him down while I tried to get close, but that cat sure put up some fight. He scratched me up pretty good but I finally managed to get the rag in his mouth and in a few minutes he passed out. I wanted to get into town before he came to and rigged up a carrying device by binding up his feet to his head with some rope and covering him with gunny sacks. I then slung him on my back with his feet and head facing away from me in case he should wake in a hurry and set out for the cabin. I had intended on loading him on my packhorse, but that cayuse wouldn't have anything to do with it, so I had to continue on into Banff on foot.

Just outside town he began to act up again and I had to unload him and give him another dose. Since he was still out cold when I hit town, I decided to have a little fun before turning him over to Norman. There's a few miners around here who I don't see eye to eye with and they tend to gather in the Alberta Bar in the late afternoon after their shift is finished. I walked into the place and pushed my way up to the bar and asked the bartender for a whiskey. "What's that on your back Bill?" he asked while he poured me a shot. I turned around so he could see and he let out a whoop, "Holy C..... boys, he's got a polecat on his back and its still breathing!" The place erupted in yells and cussing while the customers made a run for the door and that cat and I soon had the bar all to ourselves.

I finished my whiskey and Lightning and I strolled over to the zoo, where Norman and I shared a good laugh. We put the lynx in a cage by itself and watched it come around until dark. All in all, it was hard earned cash but I've sure got a good story to go with it now.

* * *

May 15
Last week while up near the ridge I saw a mother grizzly with two new-born cubs out foraging for the first time and made a mental note that if the opportunity arose I should try get them for the zoo. While down in Banff I asked Norman if the offer for cubs still held good, and he said it did and he was particularly anxious to get some. Yesterday I got my chance.

I knew Mama bear would discover my little nuisance ground down near the mine eventually, so I was keeping an eye out for her. A couple of nights ago I could hear them prowling around down there and the next day I made it even more attractive by leaving a little deer meat out. Yesterday morning on coming out of the shaft I was working, I saw the cubs on the bait and Mama not in sight. I went to the cabin and grabbed a couple of ropes with lassos that I had prepared and stuffed my knife and Colt in my belt.

I headed downslope below where they were feeding and came up at them, hoping to scare them into one or another of my shafts for protection. It worked perfectly, as they ran for the nearest dark hole, and I went in with my ropes on the ready to see if I could catch one. I could hear the little fellows squealing in the dark and I had to pause a moment to let my eyes adjust. Just then I heard a tremendous roar and knew the sow was coming on the run looking for her wayward offspring. It didn't take her a moment to pick up the scent and she headed straight for the mouth of the shaft bent on destruction. I knew the jig was up for sure if I lost my head and so very deliberately drew the Colt from my belt and waited for her to find us out. She heard the squeals and as she headed in the tunnel I took aim at her head and let go three or four rounds from the Colt.

Everything after that was a blur. My ears and head exploded from the report of the pistol in such a small space, and I remember the warm, sticky feel of blood spraying in my face mixed with the stinking smell of her breath and the gunpowder. She went down not two feet in front of me, her damn great paws clawing the air and her teeth snapping in the throes of death. I stumbled outside and got sick to my stomach, and it took several minutes before my heart stopped racing and I got my breath. In the commotion the little fellows scampered out of the tunnel and escaped down the hill, so once I regained my composure I went for my skinning knife, put a rope on her leg and skidded her out by using a tree for leverage. She was a big one and I could see that I had got her right through the eye, and therefore the brain, a bit of luck that meant it's her hide drying outside my cabin tonight and not mine.

XXI
1911

March 15
Today I decided to try my hand at a new line of work around here that bids fair to becoming a good way to beef up my grubstake a little.

Sometime ago I was talking with Howard Sibbald, the chief of the Game Guardian service that the government started here two years ago. They plan to build some trails so that the Guardians can patrol different areas of the park to nip any poaching or forest fires in the bud. Howard's a good man, the son of the old school teacher Andrew Sibbald of the McDougall Mission at Morley and a veteran of thirty years in the foothill and mountain country. But I told him there's already too many damn people traipsing around in the woods disturbing the game, and that these trails will only encourage more. He said "you can't stop progress" and suggested I look at it as an opportunity rather than a draw-back. I'm not so sure about that, but when they posted a notice at the government office for bids on a contract to clear a stretch of trail between Simpson Pass and Brewster Creek, I decided to take a kick at the cat. It might as well be me doing the work as having some other fool messing around in my territory like they have the last two years building that trail up Healy Creek to Simpson Pass.

April 24
I heard from Howard Sibbald that the government has given the trail clearing contract to Joe Boyce. He's that sneaky, no good s.o.b. who was trapping around the summit

last winter. He had no business being there as I've worked much of that territory for many years now. In fact, I became very suspicious that he was trying to break in for grub while I was out on my own line, and I took to setting a bear trap inside the door in case he got any ideas. He must have got wind of what I was up to because he never tried after that. But now he's in my hair again and taking food off my table in a different way.

Howard told me that instead of bidding on government contracts I should consider signing on with the fire and game warden service, as its now called. He said they prefer former guides and packers with lots of experience who know the country already, as well as men who haven't run afoul of the authorities for poaching. In fact, he informed me there's a position open this season and that he would support me if I write the superintendent and ask for it. I definitely fill the bill on the knowledge of the park end and have always managed to keep my poaching to myself, so while the idea of being a government man kind of sticks in my craw, being able to work out in the mountains and get paid regular for it does have some appeal.

April 26
Wrote to Superintendent Macdonald today concerning the fire and game warden postion. We'll see if they really want good men for the mountains or if they're only interested in good Liberals!

May 15
Superintendent Macdonald took my oath of office and swore me in as a justice of the peace this a.m. He then pre-

sented me with my official badge, so I guess I'm on the pub-lic purse at $3.00 a day now. It feels kind of strange, but I fig-ure it was the same when I worked on the gang for George Stewart, so I'll soon get used to the idea again. There's some tough old birds like Bob Robertson and Louis Mumford on this crew with me, and they'll be looking for me to pull my weight. But that's never been a problem with me no matter what I put my hand to.

This service has been around a couple of years now so I was more or less familiar with what I'm supposed to do even before Howard Sibbald went through it with me in detail. Our main jobs are to prevent and fight the forest fires that have too often got the best of this country and to crack down on the poaching that some of the outfits around here do while they are out on the trail but not yet out of Rocky Mountains Park. Nobody knows the nooks and crannies of this country like I do, so once I get the hang of it I'll be able to handle those duties and anything else they throw at me too.

One of the obligations of this job is to keep a daily journal of observations about weather conditions, game, work accom-plished etc., etc. Sibbald told me these must be turned in monthly and that after he reviews them they go to the superintendent and then up the line to the commissioner. I was given my first one today along with the badge, so I don't know how much I'll keep up with this journal from now on. I think I can keep the other to the basics, and since it won't be returned to me I'll still do my best to keep this one on the go when conditions allow.

May 21
So far this job reminds me much of my old days as a guide, since most of the work I've been doing in the first week has been on the end of an axe. Sibbald has had a few of us cleaning up after some of the timber cutters who took out pit props up around Inglismaldie this past winter and left the slash all over the place. It has dried out and become a fire hazard, so we're cutting it up and piling it so at least its in one place.

In a few weeks we're going to start patrolling the railroad line between Banff and Laggan on a speeder to look out for fires started by sparks from the locomotives. It's bone dry already so I can see the sense in keeping a watchful eye and it will be good to get off this business for awhile. I haven't ridden a speeder since Dave White used to take me out on little joy rides on his when he was section foreman at Sawback. It'll be good to get back in the saddle, so to speak.

June 3
I finally got off the brush piling detail, but the work hasn't got any easier. That damned government crew building the new Calgary to Banff Coach road is some careless and every time they light a fire to burn up some of the slash it gets away from them. They've been working a few miles east of Anthracite and we've been called in to help three times in the last week. This one has really taken off and its probably going to take a few days and a little wet weather to get the better of it. Between that and the hoboes who leave their campfires going when they jump their next freight, we've sure been kept hopping.

June 9

Today I put the speeder patrol theory to the test when I spotted a little conflagration near Castle Mountain while on my leg up to Laggan. I had just watched a freight with a damaged spark arrester go by a few miles back spewing all kinds of live cinders, so I was being particularly vigilant. Some of the sparks had ignited the bearberry brush alongside the right-of-way and it was already spreading into the dry grass in the meadow at Silver City when I arrived. I got busy with my shovel and mattock and began trenching around the grass, throwing the dirt I dug onto some of the hotter spots. That pretty well took care of the grass end of it, but the brush was more stubborn. Fortunately I was carrying a canvas bucket and there was a little slough close by that still had a spring freshet feeding it, so I scooped up water quickly and doused the smouldering bushes. If I had come upon it even an hour later it would likely have been a different story, as I'm pretty sure it would have raced through that grass like a herd of cayuses heading for water.

Oh well, at least I'll have something a little exciting to write up in the official diary today.

June 15

Howard had us all down to the superintendent's office on Bear Street this morning to have a little chinwag about predators. The coyotes and the odd wolf have been doing their dirty work on the deer, the sheep and some of the local henhouses for a number of years now, and its our duty to see that an end is put to their ways. We talked about dynamiting dens, the use of traps and poisoned baits as well as shooting on sight. Last fall one of the locals tried to press charges against Bob Robertson for shooting a coyote on the grounds that the carrying of guns was prohibited by the regulations. That didn't buffalo the authorities though, and they have ruled that we can carry weapons in the performance of our duties. Its a good thing too, otherwise wiping out these varmints would be near on to impossible.

I'll be hard to beat at this part of the job.

* * *

August 5
Several bears have been prowling around the Upper Hot Springs lately and yesterday we put an end to the problem. Reports from the Hydro Hotel and the Grand View Villa told of guests being scared out of their wits when meeting bruin on his nocturnal rambles and of garbage from the kitchens being scattered all over, so we had taken to increasing our patrols up there to see if we could scare them off. But lately a mother and her two cubs had become a particular nuisance and Howard told us to get rid of them. Bob Robertson and I took our rifles and went up there last evening and didn't have to wait long until they appeared. We made sure all the tourists were out of sight before we did them in, because some of them think that these pests are nothing more than cuddly, furry pets. I don't particularly like killing the young ones, but once they get bad habits they keep them for life, so the job had to be done.

August 15
We've been kept busy the past few weeks with patrols around town keeping an eye on the tourists in case they do something stupid. And believe me, they do — throwing cig-

arettes and cigars into anything that will burn, leaving campfires unattended, taking pictures of their children feeding bears, and every other imaginable brainless activity. The fact that the new road to Calgary is now open and they come in with their automobiles and run all over scaring horses and decent folk on foot doesn't help any. I don't mince my words when I see this stuff going on and Howard has told me to ease up a bit.

Yesterday, Jack Warren and myself were assigned a much more agreeable task. The powers-that-be have decided this service should have a few cabins where we can spend the night on our patrols and store fire-fighting equipment. I'd just as soon make a cold camp wherever I am at the end of the day, but that's not the way its going to be, so the crew has been assigned the job of getting out the logs for these stopover shelters. Jack and I are to start work here at the head of Goat Creek as there has been lots of trouble with the gangs from the logging camps in the Spray Valley dynamiting the fish and potting deer around Spray Lakes. We've got our camp set up now and tomorrow we'll start picking out the best of the fire-killed logs for building purposes.

August 21
Jack and I have spent the last five days cutting suitable logs for the specified fourteen by sixteen foot building, skidding them to the site with our saddle horses, and trimming and peeling them. It's been hot work and as the surroundings are somewhat swampy there's been plenty of bulldogs and mosquitoes around to keep us company.

The cabin will be one room with walls slightly over six feet high and will have a roof that projects about six feet in front of the door to provide a protected area to store wood, pack horses and perform other chores out of the weather when we are in residence. I haven't built a cabin this carefully since the one for Emily and me, but the work is enjoyable and it sure beats being traffic director for tourists.

August 28
I'm here alone at the moment as Jack has gone back to Banff to get the rest of the supplies we'll need to finish this place off. Despite frequent showers, work is progressing well on the roof, which I'm making out of dried, split logs. I should be finished by the time he gets back with a couple of pack-horses of material. He'll bring some rubberoid to cover the roof and make it waterproof as well as some shiplap for the floor and a couple of panes of glass for the windows. After we get them in, we'll cover them with shutters to deter any polecats that have a mind to come in for a visit and build a good stout door for the same purpose.

Howard Sibbald came by the other day with Sidney Vick, the Fisheries Inspector, and brought with him the first of the equipment he wants stored here, including shovels, axes, mattocks, a crosscut saw and some collapsible canvas pails. He pronounced himself very satisfied with what we've accomplished and told us that when we finish here we'll be going up to the Panther north of Banff to assist with the cabin they're about to start up there.

September 15
We've been making good progress on the Panther Creek cabin and, as this was the date that my employment was to

end for the season, I arrived back in Banff today. But when I reported to Howard at the government office, he asked if I would stay on another month or so. Although I told him I was anxious to start getting my supplies packed out for the winter, I said I would keep at it for a bit.

Howard is itching to crack down on any poaching by the hunting parties outfitting out of here this fall and sees me as a signal to them that he means business. I'll be sent out to patrol the trails these parties take going out and will seal as many weapons as possible. While I'll make myself visible when they're outbound, when they're coming back it'll be a different story. I know how to disappear in this bush and the only time they'll see me is when I drift into camp when they're least expecting it. If they've been up to no good, I'll have them dead to rights.

* * *

November 15
After a great deal of consideration, I filed yesterday on two quarter sections under the South African Veteran's grants. For the past number of years they've been distributing scrip to any veteran who wishes to take up land without the usual requirements to prove up on it. While I don't have a lot of use for more land at the moment, one is never sure when such rights might be taken away, so I decided it was in my best interest to act now. There were a couple of parcels available near my Montreal Valley place so I registered for the S. E. 1/4 and S. W. 1/4 of Section 18, Township 27, Range 5, West of the 5th. If I ever decide to go into ranching in a big way, I'm set for it now.

XXII
1912-13

September 20

Last week while on patrol near Exshaw, I ran across a shale pit that the Western Canada Coal and Cement Company had scoured out in some of their exploratory work. I poked around a bit in it, and upon moving some shattered fragments saw something interesting sticking out of the ground. A bit of excavation proved it to be a concretion of symmetrical shape with many rings and grooves, the largest "thunder egg" I've ever come across. When I was back in Banff I told Norman Sanson about it, and he said he would be interested in having it for the museum's collection.

Today I delivered it into Norman's care, but it was some job getting it here. I could see that it was too large to lift and could not convince the park to loan me a wagon in any event, so I thought about it for awhile and decided that the old Indian way of moving large loads would suffice. I made a travois out of stout poles, rolled the concretion onto it using a tree trunk and rock for leverage and then hitched it up to my horse with a piece of one of my old harnesses. It took us two days to get it into Banff, as the ground was very rough and I had to take it very slow so as not to hurt the mare. She stayed with it though, and when we got it here we manhandled it onto a large scale that Norman has and found it weighed 233 pounds. It'll make some display!

* * *

October 1
Howard has received permission from Commissioner
Harkin to keep a corps of wardens on staff over the coming
winter, and it looks like I'm to be one of them. Some of my
comrades on this service have argued that enforcing game
and poaching regulations, and sometimes being called in to
be the local dogcatcher, doesn't always make us popular in
town. They feel that if we are to accept criticisms and scowls
as part of the job, the work should be year-round and worthwhile. People's opinions are like so much water off a duck's
back to me, but I'm happy to have something that pays
steady cash given the poor returns I've had from trapping in
recent times.

October 5
Today we had a meeting to receive a new set of instructions
to wardens, which the Parks Branch has provided for our
guidance. There has been a number of instances where it
was not clear what we were supposed to do in certain situ-
ations and where some of the boys seem to have wandered
from the straight and narrow in their work. Among the
words to the wise were reminders to keep our diaries con-
scientiously, to confiscate all unsealed weapons found in the
park, to use discretion in our searching of outfits so as not to
cause undue discomfort to tourists, and to show our badges
when acting in any official capacity. The clincher though
was that anyone found intoxicated will be immediately dismissed, so we'll either see some new faces around here or a
few less red eyes in the morning!

October 17
Well, the fat's in the fire now.

We'd been hearing some rumours lately about the proposed hunting activities of none other than the genial James I. Brewster and his estimed brother-in-law Runt Moore, the former head of the game guardian service in these parts. According to our sources they had their eye on a flock of sheep in the park near the continental divide not far from my lake. Their outfit registered out about ten days ago, and this week Howard decided that he, Jack Warren and myself should take a little trip up there and see what was afoot. We were just above Bow Lake heading up to the pass when our quarry appeared in plain sight coming down the trail towards us. Having seen their camp at Bow Lake, we knew they had been working the country not far removed. Lo and behold, when we took the trouble to check under a couple of tarps they had over some packhorses, we found they had two fresh head of mutton. Jim and Phil declared their innocence, stating that the sheep had been taken over the divide in B.C., but Howard laid a charge on the spot, confiscating the carcasses and the guns before sending them on their way.

No doubt this will make for some interesting days in court and will go a long way to determining whether or not these regulations will stand up.

* * *

January 11
There's been a big cat on the prowl around here lately caus-

ing all kinds of commotion and Will Noble and I have been assigned to bring an end to his activities. Will's new on the outfit, having replaced Bob Robertson in November when he retired, and I've been given the job of showing him the ropes.

The lion has been spotted a few times around Art Jordan's lumber camp in the Spray, so that's where we've been concentrating our efforts. But these animals are nocturnal by nature and difficult to actually sight, and tracking has been made nearly impossible because the trail is constantly being obliterated with all the new snow we've been getting. We did manage to find a yearling sheep that had been killed and gutted near Goat Creek the other day, and we decided to stake it out overnight. The temperature was cold, almost 30 below, and it was no picnic sitting huddled in the dark hoping that polecat would appear. I'm sure Will was having second thoughts about his new occupation when I finally decided the cat wasn't going to show and gave the word to pull out for the Spray cabin. We'll have to get a lot luckier if we're going to nail this cat's hide to the warden barn, and I've got to admit I've got a lot of respect for any wild thing that can outsmart an old tracker like me for so long.

* * *

January 16
We've been having quite a set-to lately with the powers-that-be in Ottawa over the use of poison to keep these damn coyotes under control. As usual, they sit in their offices 3000 miles away and think they know more than the man in the field about how to do the job.

It appears the trouble started when Commissioner Harkin was reviewing my diary for November and noticed I had reported taking seven coyotes over a two day period with poison bait and number four traps, and that I also noted that another ten baits were taken a week later. Harkin has written to Howard that he doesn't wish strychnine crystals to be used because he thinks they can be eaten by other game and birds that we are trying to protect and that we should kill predators with guns only. I doubt that he'd be very happy with our success were we to do that, since getting a clear shot at a coyote in the bush and timber is a rare occurrence. Howard and I discussed the matter and today he wrote back to Harkin explaining that we've had our best success over the past couple of years with poison bait and that in any event I use only cyanide and not strychnine, since it is more likely to be left alone by non-predators. Hopefully, this will convince Mr. Harkin to keep his nose out of it and let us get on with our business.

* * *

February 25
I've been watching the situation around Castle lately with all the timber that's being cut out of there this winter for ties and pit props. These timber cutters are a cagey lot and you've got to get up early in the morning to stay ahead of them. They're not above changing the legal description of their berths on the license or straying into an adjacent berth to take out a few good logs if they think no-one is watching. There's two or three whose actions appear very suspicious to me, and as I'm taking up residence in our little shack at Castle today, I'll keep my eyes peeled for infractions.

February 28

My suspicions of a few days ago were proved out today when I snowshoed across to the north side of the Bow on my patrol. I could hear some axes at work and tracked them down to the camp of Henry Smith, who has been working in this vicinity for some time. I asked to see his permit and after hemming and hawing for a spell, he said he had forgotten it at his home in Canmore. I strongly suggested to him that he was stretching the truth, but until I can check it out with the timber registrar in Banff I'll have to hold fire.

March 6

Yesterday I finally got back to town and checked on the register of timber permits. As I suspected, Henry Smith had no berth registered on the north side of the river, his berth being about three miles south of Castle on the south side. I reported the matter to the office and then headed out here straight away and made for his camp, but there was no sign of the work I had seen going on a week ago. I went over to his registered berth and found him busy at work at this location, and when I interviewed him he said he realized he had made a mistake on the legal description of the proper berth.

He's managed to weasel out of a charge this time, but I'll be laying for him if he steps out of line again.

* * *

April 20

I've just returned from two weeks of leave spent on a grizzly hunt over in the Simpson and Mitchell River country. The bear hunting wasn't up to snuff because of the poor snow conditions, but the fossil hunting was exceptional.

I had been of the trail of a big boar for several days but kept losing him because it was impossible to determine what was old sign and new in the rotting snow. Near the Mitchell River one day I sat down against a rock in the sun to consider my next move when my eye fell on some nearby shale exhibiting an unusual colour. I went over to investigate and found numerous invertebrate fossils imbedded in the rock, so I quickly got my hammer from my pack and began to chip some of them out. One heavy blow to a particularly stubborn one loosened a big chunk of shale and upon moving it away I saw before me what looked to be a large fin. I carefully began to remove more rock and soon had exposed the fossilized skeleton of a large, square-shaped fish complete with scales and tail. It took me two hours of painstaking work to get it out whole with my heart racing all the time, as I realized I was onto the discovery of a lifetime. I got a piece of tarp to wrap it in and then placed it carefully in my best packbox, made from a Mumm's champagne case and virtually indestructible.

As the bear hunting was poor, I soon lost interest and was anxious to get my specimen to Norman Sanson for his opinion. When I arrived here the other day I took it directly over to the museum to show him, and he was as excited as I was. He thinks it is an entirely new species and wants me to allow him to send it to the National Museum to have the vertebrate paleontologist examine it. Although I had been picturing it as the centrepiece of my collection, I know he's right about its scientific importance and have allowed him to send it providing he keeps the location where I found it a secret. If I'm going to be famous, there's nothing more I'd like than it to be for such a discovery.

* * *

May 10

Howard Sibbald called us in today to introduce some of the men who have joined the outfit and to talk about how he wants to run the show this season. He'd requested seven men to join the five of us who overwintered, and was surprised when he was granted permission for five. There was a catch — ever since the change of government the candidate for any new position has to be cleared with Billy Mather and the local Conservative organization and approved by our new member, R. B. Bennett. There's some good men though — Ben Woodworth jr., Edward Tabateau, Howard Caine, Andrew Wright and Louis Hill — and with a little experience they should make the grade.

Howard wants to try something new this year by setting up districts that will have one or two men assigned to them who will patrol on a regular circuit. We'll use some of the cabins we built last year as the headquarters for these patrols and we'll build a few more this year. Howard asked me which area I'd like and, of course, I told him the Simpson Summit and Red Earth territory since I know it like the back of my hand. So I've been teamed up with Jack Bevan and we'll use the Spray cabin as a headquarters for our district, which will include the Spray and Kananaskis valleys to White Man's Pass, Mount Assiniboine, and the Simpson Summit including the Healy Creek and Brewster Creek drainages. Howard asked if we could use the Bookrest cabin as a temporary shelter this year until a more permanent one is built to use in the patrol of that part of the district, and I've agreed providing a new one is constructed soon.

* * *

August 11
When I signed on with this outfit I was prepared to do anything they asked me, but I never thought it would be picking flowers.

For the past month I've been helping off and on with the great heather gathering expedition. Early in July, Mr. Knechtel, the Chief Forester of Dominion Parks, appeared in Banff with instructions to collect a quantity of some suitable flowering plant to be included in a small pamphlet on the park that the department intends to issue next year. Norman Sanson has been deputized entirely to this work and as he and Mr. Knechtel decided the best location to pursue it was around Simpson Pass, I was directed to help as well. After a careful reconnaisance, they decided that the red and purple heather that grows in profusion in the meadows at this time of the year would fit the bill.

We've been using the Bookrest as heather headquarters for the most part and we've dried, pressed and put up large quantities. Knechtel now believes the book should be called "Just A Sprig Of Mountain Heather" and I'll pack him and the first load out to Banff tomorrow, as he must now return to Ottawa. Norman and his assistant, Hughie Sibbald, are going to stay and collect more and I'll come back to pitch in when my duties allow.

September 10

I ran into A. O. Wheeler today when he was in town resup-
plying the bacon and beans for his survey work. He's been
doing some measuring of the peaks along the divide as part
of this boundary survey between Alberta and British
Columbia that they started this summer. Wheeler's the
British Columbia representative and his job is to determine
the altitude of the mountains while Mr. Cautley, the Alberta
representative, ties in the passes and places the boundary
markers in them. Wheeler informed me that Cautley will be
moving from the Vermilion Pass, where he has been working, to the Simpson Pass in a few days and that part of his
instructions are to tie in any mining claims with the boundary work. That means the Bookrest, and I think I better get
my hide out there to see what's going on if I can get Howard
to let me patrol that area for a few days.

September 12

Yesterday I convinced Howard to let me go to see what's
happening up at my claim — I'm damn sure I don't want
any government types running amok there while I'm not
around. I've put too much sweat and blood into the
Bookrest now to have anything go wrong, just when I'm
beginning to see my way clear to get some good ore out of
there.

The weather has been miserable for the last few days with
several inches of snow at Banff every morning. As I made
my way on the mare up Healy Creek it became deeper and
about noon I ran into a forlorn looking chap coming down
on foot and I stopped to talk to him. It seems that he was Mr.
Cautley's cook, and he told me there was so much snow up

on top and he was so fed up that he didn't intend on going back. He also told me that Cautley lost some of his survey equipment in the Vermilion River moving camp. I suspected I wouldn't find him in the best of humour, which was indeed the case. In a weak moment I took pity on him and his assistant and brought them up to the mine to thaw out and get themselves organized. But there was also method in my madness because it gave me a chance to dig out the information I wanted on their intentions. Cautley thinks my claim is on the Alberta side of the divide and therefore in the park, rather than the B.C. side. If that's so it will be bad news and will put me in a real pickle the way they've taken to changing the regulations in the last few years.

September 13
Cautley has now run a few preliminary lines and told me he is convinced the mine is in the park. He said that his instructions required him to mark it on the map the boundary survey is producing, so the fat will soon be in the fire.

Wheeler and his crew are supposed to be about in a few days as they are working on their triangulation just to the west of here. I've always found him to be a fair man, although somewhat opinionated and a bit superior in the way he conducts the Alpine Club. However, he knows the situation as well as anyone and I'll need some help if I'm going to win this battle.

September 16
Wheeler and his men arrived in my camp yesterday and are staying a few days while they take on the peaks they need to climb for their triangulation work. One of his helpers is

Conrad Kain, an Austrian climbing guide I met about three years ago, who tells me he led the party that recently made the ascent of Mount Robson at the Alpine Club camp. For a climbing guide Conrad is a good sort as he stays in Canada all year around and has spent some time prospecting and trapping, so we had some interesting stories to share. He asked me how things were going and I'm afraid that Cautley's recent pronouncement had put me in rather a morose state as I found myself confiding in him how much I miss Emily and how nothing much seems to really matter in this life since she left. I ended by giving him a good piece of advice if he intends on living a life in the mountains — depend on no-one but yourself, keep your own counsel, and be prepared to meet this country on its own terms!

September 18
This morning before he pulled out to move on towards Mount Assiniboine, Wheeler and I had an opportunity to have a serious chinwag. He said he understood my predicament and felt that some allowance should be made for the fact that I was working these digs before the park boundary was extended in 1902. He agreed to talk to Ottawa about my case and see if something couldn't be worked out. I hope he's successful because while this warden business is going well for the moment, one never knows when he's going to need to return to his old ways for a livelihood.

XXIII
1914

January 7

I guess I caused quite a stir at headquarters when they read last August's diary entry on my discovery of trap rock at Simpson Summit. This rock is a dark colour and, as it is of volcanic origin, is very unusual in these mountains, which are sedimentary. The only other outcropping of igneous rock I have come across is in the Bow Valley north of Laggan, and it is very small. Back in October, Commissioner Harkin wrote the superintendent to instruct him to have me bring in some samples of the rock, which the department feels might be valuable for road construction purposes. I forgot to do so before the snow flew, but because Harkin has brought the matter up again Mr. Clarke had me write a report on the discovery today.

In my report I told Harkin I followed the outcropping for several miles and found it continuous, crossing the CPR line not far from Castle Siding. It is found between Cambrian formations, but I could not tell whether it was from over-flow during the Cambrian period or the filling of a fissure at a later time. I concluded by promising to send samples to Ottawa this spring when the ground clears.

* * *

February 4

Howard spoke to me today about the activities of the section men along the line between Banff and Laggan. We've suspected for some time that they've been poaching deer. There are large numbers of the animals congregating along the track and these men, who are mainly foreigners and come and go regularly, Howard believes are ignorant of the game and park regulations. I'm not so kind in my opinion — I think they know them very well but just don't give a damn.

Last year when we had new fire and game signs printed outlining the regulations, we took the trouble to have some made up in foreign languages, including Polish, to try address this matter. It's been to no avail, so now we're to start cracking down.

February 9
As instructed, I've been keeping an eagle eye on the section men and yesterday I hit paydirt. I charged one J. Karigor, a section man at Sawback Siding, with poaching a deer.

Without him knowing, I'd been periodically watching from the woods for the last few days. In the middle of the afternoon, I saw him leave the sectionhouse with what appeared to be a rifle wrapped in a tarp and head west on a handcar. Not being so equipped myself, I had to snowshoe down the right-of-way and about an hour later heard him approaching, so had to duck into the bush. It looked like he had something on the handcar under the tarp, but I couldn't be sure as he went by quickly and it was beginning to snow. I continued west about another half-mile and came upon some tracks leading from the line up the side of the mountain. Although they were beginning to disappear in the snow, I managed to follow them for several hundred yards before noticing a bit of blood under a tree. It was fresh, so I started to do a search for evidence, working out in circles from the location of the blood. Something caught my eye in a tuft of moss, and I brushed away the dusting of snow to expose a 22 short shell casing.

Evidence in hand, I hightailed it back to the sectionhouse and, seeing no-one, went right in. Karigor was not about, but there was a haunch of fresh venison on the table and a rifle similar to that which had fired the shell leaning against the wall. I smelled the breach and could tell it had been fired recently. I went outside to see if I could find my culprit and there he was just stepping out of the outhouse hitching up his pants. He almost dropped them again in his astonishment at seeing me standing there!

February 15
Appeared before Magistrate Tom Wilson today to give evidence in the case against Karigor. We had him dead to rights, even though he tried to argue he'd been given the meat by another railway worker. Tom found him guilty and fined his $50.00 and costs of $3.95. Howard was delighted and is going to ask the superintendent to take the matter up with the CPR brass to try put an end to this business.

* * *

September 20
The talk here lately has been of nothing but the war and how many are joining up. Cyril Child and some of the others around here have formed a Banff Corps of Guides and have all volunteered in the hope that it will be kept together in some unit. When the fireworks started I figured it was a younger man's game, but with each day the news of the

fighting in Europe is making me more uneasy and I feel just like I did when I read about the Boer War. Today I made up my mind to throw in my lot with the boys rushing to the colours and told Howard I would be leaving. He asked me to reconsider at first, but when he saw I was determined he extended his congratulations on my patriotism.

September 26
Confound those recruiting officers. I've been down in Calgary trying to join up and have visited two recruiting offices with the same result. They ask me my age and after the doctor has a look at my Boer War wound they say they are looking for younger and sounder men. It doesn't seem to matter that I'm fitter than a mountain lion or wilier than a coyote — they say rules are rules. I'm going to head for the Bookrest for the moment and give it another try later.

XXIV
1915-16

May 6

As I suspected, with the war going on longer than anybody expected and the recent Canadian casualties in Belgium, the newspapers have been calling on those with experience up to forty-five years old to step forward. Yesterday I managed to convince a recruiting officer in Calgary that I'm younger than my teeth would make me appear and they decided to take me on. Must be desperate I guess, but Lance- Corporal Peyto it is. I've joined the 12th Canadian Mounted Rifles under Colonel George Macdonald and I won't lack for company with Will Noble, Arthur Unwin, Jack Lowery and few other Banff lads present and accounted for. Phil Moore was our second-in-command up until a short time ago, but he was rewarded for his hard work and his training at the Royal Military College in Kingston with a promotion to Brigade Major with the Western Infantry Brigade in Winnipeg.

May 11

They figure that with my warden background I'll make a good weapons man. We're now training at a camp they've established on the edge of the Sarcee Indian Reservation at Calgary. We're using the Ross Rifle, but I've told them that damn thing is only good for target practice and that it's bound to get a few good blokes killed if they stick with it for the real action. I've put in for machine gun training because I'm not the cavalryman I was in my South Africa days and I figure I've got a better chance of making it through this mix-up behind a machine gun than with a Ross. I hear that Sam

Hughes, the Minister of Militia in charge of the Canadian Expeditionary Force, is insisting on the Ross because it's Canadian-made. It sounds like the same kind of pig-headed thinking that got us into such trouble with the British generals on the veldt. We hear rumours that some of the units who took part in the battle at Ypres in April found them so inadequate that they have found a way to re-equip with the new Lee Enfields. I used a 306 Lee Enfield on my predator work the last few years and they are a much superior weapon.

May 18

I began my machine gun training a few days ago and although it takes a little getting used to I'm beginning to get the hang of it. It's a Vickers water-cooled recoil weapon that takes two men to operate, one feeding the belts of ammunition while the other does the shooting, so its a lot like packing where teamwork is a must. My partner is a rancher about my age — I guess they figured they better put the old dogs together so we wouldn't loose patience with all these young pups around here who don't know a gun barrel from a hole in the ground. Lord knows Fritz is going to make mincemeat out of them unless they can get savvy before they ship out.

I've been having some trouble with one of my fingers that got all bent up a few years back when it got caught in the pack ropes of a bucking cayuse. I had the doctor look at it and he said the end of it was going to have to come off if I was going to be a machine gunner, because it was useless and would get in the way. The surgeon wanted to put me out while he did the work but I told him no. When he asked why, I said I wanted to watch him do it in case I ever had to do it myself! It hurt like Hell but they've got it all bandaged and doctored up now, so I'll never miss it in a few days.

May 23
The training continues to go well and me and my mate George Busby are about the best in the unit — who says you can't teach old dogs new tricks! We're not sure when we'll be shipped out because we still need a lot of work before we'll survive in the gas, the mud and the artillery we hear about. Despite what we read in the papers the trenches in Belgium and France apparently have a big appetite and from the rumours we here our boys over there are being chewed up and spit out faster than the British Army can ask for another helping, so it probably won't be too long.

May 27
A. O. Wheeler was in town the other day so he took time to come out to the Sarcee camp for a little visit. I've picked up an old set of false teeth and I was doing a little carving on them when he came by. He's been doing his best I know about the Bookrest business, but he had to tell me it doesn't look good as the government's sticking to its guns about hauling any ore out of there. Damn those Ottawa s.o.b.s, why can't they just leave a man alone to try make a living when he's not bothering anybody or anything.

* * *

November 1
I had a few days of furlough so I went out to Banff to settle a few things and say good-bye to some of my pals. I board-

ed up the house and asked Dave White and Norman Sanson to take care of everything worth stealing. In return I said it was theirs if I don't come back. It reminded me of when I left for South Africa, but that seems like a lifetime ago and I sure had a better feeling about it than I do for this.

November 15
I've just spent six days packed on a colonist car and I now know how a steer feels when he's being shipped to market. We've arrived in Halifax and are to board a troop ship in the next few days, not an altogether pleasant prospect when I consider the winter storms and the German submarines we'll probably meet out on the Atlantic.

Although we were told when we left Calgary that we wouldn't be able to keep any diaries when we got overseas, I decided to keep a few notes on scraps of paper when the higher-ups aren't watching for transfer to this journal later. I always regretted not doing that in South Africa despite the orders, and so I'll keep the little bit I can in secret.

From what we hear we'll be doing more training when we get to England and will probably become part of the rumoured new Third Division with other units that are headed in the same direction as us. We apparently will be under the command of General M. S. Mercer who has a good reputation.

December 10
Our voyage was not as difficult as I thought it would be — we hit a few good waves but no hostiles. Thank God! When we arrived we were given six days leave and many of us

who hailed from these parts spent the time with our families. I went out to Welling, where I had not been since I was returning home from South Africa fifteen years ago. I stayed with my youngest sister, Maria, who is now married to a fine chap and has a growing family. In was nice to be with them but as the children are about the same age as my own dear Robin it added to my melancholy as well. Mother was there and is very elderly now, but she still has all her wits about her and asked me many questions about some of the things which I've written to her.

After our furlough we took the train to Bramshott Camp, where we have begun our training anew. We should be good fighters in wet weather because it rains every day. We hear that we'll probably get leave again for Christmas, so I'll head back for London and a few drinks with some of the boys.

* * *

January 1
Happy New Year for what its worth. Had a good old time in London at Christmas but what a God-forsaken place for a celebration Bramshott Camp is. They've had us training every day on our bayonet charges, practicing with dummy grenades or doing interminable target practice with the Ross. Each day is the same and it sure gets me down. When we're not training we're sitting around in the old ramshackle huts we're billeted in, with all twenty-five of us trying to keep warm around a coal stove in the middle. Our beds are thin six foot long planks and they have us stacked up like dried fish. I'd prefer to be over there face to face with

the Germans rather than sitting here waiting — I never was much good for that.

The news we get isn't very good and I suspect they are only telling us the half of it. Some of these young boys are scared stiff, although they try to put on a brave face. I try to help by telling them some of the stories about the jackpots I've survived with rampaging rivers and raging grizzlies and about how we learned to keep our hides out of the sights of the sharpshooting Boers. But most of them think I'm just a raving old timer, a bit touched in the head, so lately I've taken to keeping my own counsel.

February 26
I'm still stuck in England but have been moved to a better camp at Shorncliffe, where most of the Canadians are training. This was occasioned by the smashing up of our regiment, with our lads going to just about every other Canadian unit. Most of the 12th went with the 8th and 9th CMRs to be made into a new infantry battalion — what a terrible fate for good stout-hearted cavalrymen. I was a bit luckier because of my good sense in taking machine gun training, as I have been assigned to the 37th Battalion in the machine gun section. The only problem is that we're a reserve battalion, so I still have no idea when I'll get into the fray.

* * *

March 26
Word has it that we're headed for the Ypres salient to provide reinforcement to the Second Division. Ypres is a west

Belgian town that was not taken in the first push by the Germans in 1914 and is connected to our front by a little bulge in the German lines. It has been defended by Canadians for the past year and it was there that the First Division saw action last April and suffered over 6,000 casualties in the process. Hopefully these Canadian generals that Hughes has put in command have learned something since then so we don't meet the same fate.

April 10
We reached Le Havre a week ago and were immediately boarded onto small French trains that took us directly into Steenvorde in Belgium. This is somewhat behind the main lines and allowed us a few days to get used to the surroundings, which are pretty bleak. We billeted anywhere we could, usually in barns, while the officers took up residence in the farmhouses. Yesterday they brought us up to the M and N trenches on the south flank of the salient, an area that is quiet at the moment and is used to get the new boys familiar with the terrain and trench life. We don't know for sure, but we think we'll be moved up to the front soon.

April 21
We're at the front now and for the past little while the action has been heavy. A few days ago the Tommies set Fritz back on his heels when they successfully tunneled under one of the major hills around here, called Messines Ridge, and set off seven mines which created huge craters. They then occupied these craters and so far have successfully defended them, although the Germans are pulling out all the stops to try capture them.

We are busy defending the English boys' flank and trying to hold up our part of this God-forsaken piece of mud. An old trail hand like me can sleep anywhere there's ground and a rock to lay his head on, but you have to catch your winks when it's not too dangerous, which usually means during the daytime. At night we're either out on patrols ourselves in no man's land between us and the German barbed wire, or are on the look-out for German patrols while we try to repair our trenches and wire. A lot of the real action takes place just at dawn and dusk, so we have to be particularly watchful then. The artillery fire goes on and off with no apparent rhyme or reason and at night the Germans send up flares to light the show for their machine gunners. Everyone is afraid that the enemy will launch another gas attack like they did a year ago.

I'm constantly hungry and always feel like I did on the trail back down the Saskatchewan in '98 when we only had a can of sardines to eat. The rations are bully beef, tea, bread and jam, but there are never enough and anything that is left lying around falls victim to the huge rats that roam the trenches. But I prefer them to the body lice, which sometimes drive me crazy. When things are quiet everyone spends much of their time "reading their shirts" trying to get rid of these damn itchy little varmints. When the action quiets down enough we get to fall back behind the lines for a rest, a bath and a disinfecting of our underwear, but that has happened rarely lately.

May 26
Things have been pretty calm for some days now as we have been defending the Ypres - Comines - Canal - Messines front along the salient's south flank, and I finally have a chance to

catch up on this record. Little has changed from my previous description, except that George and myself have seen some real action now. A few nights ago during a German patrol we had our machine-gun dugout in a shell hole that was right in the line of their advance, and we let go on them when they were least suspecting it. We had them pinned down for about half-an-hour and our gun was kept busy all the time — while you can never be sure I think our work was pretty deadly. Killing is never a pleasant task, but its that or be killed out here and it was these Germans who started the whole thing and deserve whatever we can give them.

June 1
Today I've seen death and carnage on a terrible scale — it seems like one of those horrible dreams I used to have of a grizzly chewing me up in camp at night. Someone who's lived as hard a life as I shouldn't be bothered by anything, but then I could never imagine a scene like this.

We've been expecting a big German push for awhile now, and today it came with a vengeance. We're near Hooge, a little Belgian town where we are defending the strategic Meny road and a little ways away from the main point of a monster German artillery attack on Mount Sorrel. The ground shook constantly all day and I saw bodies being hurled into the air mixed with mud and whole trees as the relentless barrage continued. Later in the day we could see German infantry wreaking havoc in our lines defending the ridge, and it's certain that the whole Third Divison has been badly bloodied.

Just while I was writing this, word has come down the line that our C. O., Major-General Mercer, has been killed in the attack. It's a dark day indeed.

* * *

July 26
This is the first day that I've felt well enough to take up writing again. Life has never been easy, and the last two weeks have been among the worst.

On June 2nd, a day after my last entry, I came as close to making the acquaintance of the Grim Reaper as I ever care to. The day began with a counter-attack by General Currie on Mount Sorrel, which, I found out later, failed to take it from the Germans. The artillery barrage was intense in our sector and George and I were on our gun constantly throughout the day. Early in the afternoon it started to plug with mud, a not unusual occurrence, and I got up from our dug-out to clear the breach. Just as I rose an incoming round exploded just to the side of us, throwing deadly shrapnel in our direction. I was between George and the shell and caught a big piece in the right thigh, ripping away a piece of flesh the size of my hand. In thinking about it later, if I had not got up at that precise moment the shrapnel would have taken me in the head and I would not be alive to contemplate my luck.

George had suffered a wound in the upper abdomen and after taking care of him as best I could I managed to get a field dressing on my leg. We could do nothing then but lay low and grit our teeth because it was impossible for ambulance men to get to us in the heat of the battle. Eventually the bombardment lifted enough for me to attract the attention of some stretcher-bearers, but as George was in worse condition than me I told them to take him first. Right afterwards things got hot again and after a few hours I realized that I was going to have to take matters into my own hands.

Myself and another lad in my unit, who had also been winged, set off for the rear and help. I crawled on my stomach through the slop dragging my useless leg behind me with machine-gun rounds sweeping the ground all around us. We made our way as best we could from one trench to another, gradually removing ourselves from the worst area of conflict. Slipping into one trench, we were met by the most pitiable sight I have ever seen — a young soldier had received a wound that had completely mangled his leg, which was caught under a heavy gun, and he was bravely attempting to sever it with his own knife. Our own state of shock and his screams of pain at first completely unnerved us, but we regained our senses and took over the task, amputating the useless limb as efficiently as we could. I've cut many a haunch off a sheep or deer, and I tried to keep in mind how to do it and blank out the fact that it was a human being and not game that I was working on. The next ambulance man we encountered we directed to this poor lad and continued to move towards the rear as best we could on our own steam. Eventually we were gathered up by stretcher-bearers and I finally had the wound properly dressed twenty-four hours after receiving it.

I was kept at a field hospital in France for three days, and although I was sometimes delirious with pain I know that I was given excellent treatment under difficult conditions for the medical personnel. The food was also a great improvement on that I had enjoyed in the trenches. I was then evacuated to England and a hospital at Sheffield and finally to the convalescent home at Ludgate Lane, where I am now. They are caring for me well and I have no cause for complaint for there are many far worse off than me.

August 19
I've recently been moved to the King's Convalescent Home at Busby Park near London to continue my rehabilitation. They placed me here because it has many beds paid for by Canadian funds. I didn't give much thought to the money-raising efforts of the various patriotic funds in Banff before joining up, but I can certainly see their worth now. I am being treated very well and am making good progress, so I hope to be strong enough to go back into the line before too long.

September 25
Just when I thought this damn thigh had healed up pretty good I got an infection and the wound got as bad again as it originally had been. I was in a great deal of pain and danger so they moved me here to the Moore Barracks Hospital about three weeks ago. I can remember very little but the nurse told me I am lucky to be alive — she said I was as tough as they come and she's right too.

I'm feeling much better today and when she came into dress my wound she commented that she couldn't understand why the men in the hospital, despite carrying wounds like mine or even missing limbs, wanted to get back in the line. She pointed to one poor bloke in a wheelchair and said,

"Why would he want to go back?" I said, "Because he thinks he knows who did it."

But joking aside, I'm anxious to give Fritz more medicine than I was able to in the couple of months of action I had. I'm to go in front of a medical review board in the next few days and they'll decide if I'm fit for duty.

October 11
The medical board has made their review and the decision is not favourable. They say my leg has a long way to go yet, and combined with my age I am not a good prospect for quick rehabilitation. Despite my arguments, they have ordered me invalided home. They say that if I improve greatly there and this dirty war lasts long enough, I'll be able to serve again. I'm shipping out tomorrow, so I guess I might as well make the best of it.

* * *

November 6
After a long and tiring sea voyage and a very tedious passage on the train, I arrived back in Banff last night. How good it was to be heading west into the mountains in the moonlight and hear the conductor's familiar refrain. "Banff . . . Banff is the next stop."

When I got off the train it was long past midnight and I had to walk down to the house, as the hotel busses had stopped running for the season. I tried to find where I had buried the key in the moonlight, but couldn't remember the exact spot. I considered going across the road to Walter's and waking he and Rosabelle up, but decided that I had slept in far worse places than my shed over the last few years and bunked in there instead. This morning I went over to Walter's and walked in in the middle of their breakfast — they were sure happy to see me and we had a long confab as there was much to catch up on.

November 9

I've been home for a few days now and the melancholy that bothered me so much after Emily's death has returned. The leg's been bothering me, waking me up at night and aching just about all day. If it doesn't get a lot better I'm going to be about as useless as a one-legged grizzly. What good is a mountain man who can't get into the mountains? They're still paying me my $1.10 a day army pay while I recover, but what will I do to keep body and soul together when that runs out?

When I looked around the place yesterday I noticed that my neighbours had taken objection to the naming of my abode. I admit it's a bit ramshackle and before the war I had put a new sign out — "Tumble Down." In my absence two new signs appeared on either side — "Tumble Inn" and "Tumble Out." Given my recent humour I didn't rightly appreciate their point, so I spent a couple of hours fashioning a new one and then managed to crawl up the ladder to hang it out. It reads "Ain't it Hell."

XXV
1916-17

December 12

The leg's been faring somewhat better lately and I'm beginning to feel like a whole man again. If things keep on improving I'll be able to get out to the Bookrest before long.

I've been talking to Walter about the future of the warden service — he was taken on in 1914, stayed with it right through the war, and is one of the few that they keep on year-round. Before I signed up Howard Sibbald told me that they would give preference to returned men when things settled down again. I'll have to see how I feel when this bum leg comes around.

I'm not sure I'd want to be wearing the badge right now anyway with all the bad feeling about the crack down on poaching and the searching of residents' houses for illicit game. My old pal Jim Simpson seems to be taking the brunt of it, because he was convicted on three counts in a trial the other day. Apparently he took a couple of sheep out on the west road in November and Howard, Jack Warren and brother Walter found him out and tracked the evidence to his house.

January 3

It's a new year and after remembering how bad the last one was I think I better start looking ahead rather than brooding on the past. I'm going to start with a trip into the Bookrest. While the leg is far from perfect I think I can muster enough to get me there and Jim Simpson is going to come along to help out and get away from the bad publicity. We may even put out a few sets if the spirit moves us.

January 7
Well, I managed to make it in here, hobbling like a wounded coyote. The weather was way below zero when we started out and Jim tried to convince me several times to give it up, but I knew if I didn't make it now I could forget about it for a long time. At the point we turned away from the creek to head up toward the pass the snow was knee deep and I was starting to feel the pain real good. Looking at my tracks I could tell I was dragging one snowshoe pretty bad, but Jim was ahead breaking trail so he couldn't see.

When we got to the place I went right in to rest a moment while Jim gathered some wood for the fire. It looked like no-one had been messing around in here during my absence as everything was pretty much as I remembered leaving it — even my little animal house was still sitting on the bunk. It smelt a bit musty and so I started taking out the windows and propped open the door. Jim cussed me roundly, muttering why anyone needed to air out a cabin when it was 40 below outside was beyond him, but, as usual, I ignored him. Tomorrow I'll start checking out the shafts to see if anyone's been snooping around in there.

Lord, it's good to be back here. I can't count the times that thinking about this place kept me going in the trenches and while I lay rotting in hospital. I think it saved my sanity.

January 9
I went over to look at the new place I was working on before

the war and note the warden service made few improvements in my absence. It was to be mainly for winter patrol work and, as I was to build it to my own needs, I used a vertical log design and put a skylight in to get some sun in during the short hours of light. Tex Wood took over this district after my departure, but it doesn't look like he gave this place so much as a look-see. He probably spent all his time down at the district cabin on Healy Creek we built in 1914. I never did like the location of that place as you can't see who's coming or going from there, but Tex must have found its proximity to town to his liking.

* * *

June 4
Lately I've been trying to convince the superintendent to recognize my rights to take some ore out of the Bookrest, but it's no use. He doesn't seem interested in my argument that someone who put his life on the line for King and Country and now is crippled because of it should get a bit of consideration. I have no choice but to abandon my efforts there, at least for the moment, and try some other prospects.

The ones I've got my eye on are the talc deposits that lie in the banks of that little stream draining towards Egypt Lake, near Redearth Pass. I first discovered them many years ago and admired the beautiful soft cream-coloured steatite talc that lay in beds visible everywhere. I didn't think much about them again until the time I wanted a stone for Emily's grave and they came to mind. Back in those days the only use of talc I had seen was for Indian soapstone carvings, but now it is being bought commercially for making powdered talc and for carvings in the curio trade.

Although I don't know much about it yet, I'm doing a bit of reading to bone up. My only fear is that, like the Bookrest, these deposits are located very close to the park boundary. I don't want to get caught in a jackpot like that again.

July 1
What a glorious day! Not only is it our country's birthday, but it also marks the first day I've spent with my son in eleven years.

I've always intended to go over to Armstrong and have some time with Robin, but something always interfered. Miss McCleary married a fellow named Logan soon after Robin went to live there, and as the boy was still very young he quickly began to think of him as his father. Although I missed him, I thought I should leave well enough alone, but in recent times he's taken to asking questions so we arranged for him to spend part of the summer with me.

Even though they've got their hands full with that new baby, Walter and Rosabelle have agreed to have Robin bunk in with them. My place isn't really fit for a youngster his age and they want him to get to know his young cousins — Walter, Stan and Syd. But he needs to spend as much time as possible with me and hopes I'll teach him how to ride. I just wish this leg was a bit better so I could show him a few of my old tricks. But no matter, we're going to have a wonderful time together and get to know each other.

July 7

Robin and I arrived at the talc beds today and have pitched camp at the little lake nearby. We brought two saddle horses and one pack animal for our tent and grub. It was a rough ride for me — I had to keep one leg out of the stirrup and get off often to work the stiffness out. The boy did just fine and felt like a real man when I let him lead the packhorse most of the way.

After we made camp I took him over to show where the best talc deposits were and where I had cut out his mother's headstone. Later, as we sat around the campfire, he began to ask questions about her, and for the first time it hit me that he was too young to remember her when she died. I told him all about her cheerful ways and her love of getting into the mountains when she could, and that seemed to please him. Now, as I sit in the tent and write this, I look over at him sleeping and can clearly see something of Emily in his dark hair and eyes. It's almost like looking at a ghost and the terrible sense of loss that haunted me for so many years after her death is returning. It will be a long night.

July 11

We've spent the last four days drilling at various locations to find the best of these deposits. At one spot I worked all yesterday and found the bed to be almost five feet thick! Through this process I've identified a large area of interest and this afternoon Robin and I began to stake it out so that it can be registered. I'm going to take several samples to be assayed and although I'm not yet sure how I'll get the stuff out of here, I'm certain that it's a valuable find.

Robin has been a great help and is not afraid of a little work. When we're not busy prospecting, I've spent the last few days reading to him from this journal and telling him a few tales about my life. He says that he has read some boys' adventure books but the stories in them don't hold a candle to mine. I can see that he's a chip off the block and now that most of the work is done I've promised to show him how to handle the Colt. He tells me that he likes school, but not everything can be learned in a classroom, so for this summer at least I'll be his teacher.

July 27
Today Robin and I arrived in Windermere, B.C. to register my talc claim, as this is the headquarters for the mining district in which it lies. I've decided to call it the Red Mountain Claim as it sits at the head of Red Earth Creek. I also staked an adjoining claim, which I've called the Black Diamond, in Walter's name.

Our journey over here from Banff was sure delightful. I decided to use it as an excuse for a little camping trip and we made our way leisurely down the Vermilion and Kootenay Rivers and through Sinclair Canyon into the Columbia Valley. We stopped at many old fishing spots I know along the way and have been feeding regular on the bull trout we've taken. Its been a great opportunity to get to know my boy better, and I just wish this happy life could last a little longer. But we've got to mount up and head back for Banff on the double quick tomorrow, because he's due to head home in early August. I already know I'll miss him greatly.

August 2

I put Robin on the train today after we promised each other that we would spend more time together. It reminded me of when he first left in Annie White's arms, but I'm feeling a lot better about the future now than I did then. He's quite a little man and easy to be proud of. Last night he came right out and asked if I would ever marry again. It caught me by surprise, coming from one so young, and I didn't really answer, but on considering it today I think he was really trying to tell me it would be alright with him if I did.

XXVI
1920

May 12
After a long spell cogitating on the matter, I've decided to take Howard Sibbald up on his offer to rejoin the ranks of the warden service. He tells me that I'm about the best one he ever had and there's been a real push lately to give returned men government jobs. I'm on an army pension now but it's not enough to keep body and soul together so I can sure use a steady income. Walter's delighted and claims that the Peyto boys will leave their mark on this outfit.

Howard told me I could have my old district back and it'll be mighty good to get out to some of my favourite haunts again.

May 17
There's been a bushel of changes around here in the years since I handed in my badge to go off to war. We're still supposed to patrol trails, build cabins, shoot predators and clamp down on poachers as in the past, but there's been a couple of modern inventions that I'm going to have to get savvy about.

We already had a new gasoline pump that could be mounted on a speeder for fire-fighting purposes in 1914 and they took delivery of a complete fire-fighting auto in 1915, but there's been lots of new and better equipment added since then. We now have a total of five pumps along with the auto and last year they took on the grandaddy of them all — a Reo fire-fighting truck with pump capable of handling several thousand feet of hose and delivering 130 gallons of water per minute at 120 pounds pressure. That should make a big dent in any fires we're fighting around town or along the road, but it won't help much in the bush. They want all the wardens to be able to drive these rigs, but there's no way this old cowboy is going to get behind the wheel of one of those contraptions. I've already watched a couple of the boys come to grief in the Indian Days grounds as they tried to master that art.

The other "improvement" around here is the telephone system that the superintendent has been pushing for a number of years. The idea is to link all the district cabins so that we can keep in contact with each other to report any fires, poaching etc. Its a very simple single wire system that's supposed to be strung between the trees at about fifteen feet using porcelain insulators. It sounds like a Hell of a lot of work for very little use to me, because any warden who is in his cabin talking on the set isn't out doing his real job combing every inch of his district.

However, I've been informed that it's now part of the deal to learn how to handle the smaller fire pumps and to use and repair the telephone system, so it looks like having passed my fiftieth birthday I'm to go back to school.

June 1
They've been teaching me the ropes with these new pumps down at the river every day and I'm finally getting the hang of it. Today we lit a small fire of branches and debris to give it a real test, and it worked fine, but that was at the same grade as the water source. I don't think it will be the same

case when we have to run a couple of hundred feet of hose up a hill or over a ridge, so I'll be a Doubting Thomas until I see it in real action.

That probably won't be too long off, since this is one of the driest and windiest springs I can ever remember. It's like a tinder box around here and it won't take but one wayward cigarette or good lightning strike to get these woods going real good.

June 15
I moved into the Healy Creek cabin about a week ago to get going on my district patrols for the season. Although I helped build this place back in '14, I never stayed in it then and don't rightly enjoy it now. It's down in the bottom of the valley in the trees next to the water, which makes seeing or hearing anything nigh on to impossible. If anyone going past is following the trail it'll be fine, but anyone up to no-good won't be on the trail and can easily sneak past. I've been scouting around for a better look-out and have decided the top of the cliff right behind the cabin fits the bill perfectly. I'll build myself a little shelter up there and put in a line to haul things on. No-one is going to pull the wool over Warden Peyto's eyes.

* * *

August 8
We've been kept busy lately putting out small fires that have broken out due to carlessness with campfires in the extremely dry conditions we've been experiencing, but until today nothing big has been reported. However, early this morning

word was received of a fire in the Simpson River area from some Alpine Clubbers who'd been at camp at Mount Assiniboine. Tex Wood was sent out from Banff and stopped to pick me up on his way up Healy Creek. We figured that to size this thing up we needed a good vantage point and I decided that down towards the Simpson from the Bookrest would be a good one if the reports were accurate.

When we got near the lake at the foot of The Monarch the smoke was thick as a blanket and we could hear the fire roaring like a locomotive, so we knew she was a big one. While fires over in B.C. are not our responsibility, we knew that this one could easily come into the park, most likely over Citadel Pass into Howard Douglas Creek, and given the conditions that would spell trouble. We hightailed it back to Banff and looked up Howard to give him the news. I'll stay over here tonight while a decision is made on what to do.

August 9

Because we're spread so thin, the superintendent has contacted the authorities to get permission to use the Mounted Police "A" Division squadron from Fort McLeod, training down at the end of the golf links, to assist us with fire-fighting. By noon we had twenty good men organized and ready to go along with our two best packhorses to carry in the pumps and the hose. Although the going will be pretty rough, we'll try to take the outfit up Howard Douglas Creek and then come down on the fire from Citadel Pass. Tonight we're camped at the confluence of Brewster and Howard Douglas Creeks and at first light we'll bushwack our way up to the pass and survey the situation.

August 12
I've been too busy to write as this fire has kept us hopping
for the past few days. Tex and I decided to establish our base
camp at the bottom of Porcupine Hill and try to fight the fire
from both sides. The pumps worked reasonably well down
in the valley bottom, but up on the slopes we had to cut
some lines and backfire wherever possible. The Mounted
Police boys were excellent recruits — young and strong and
used to taking orders and carrying them out with no questions asked. At one point four of five of them were dis-
patched back up on the pass as the fire was creeping over
into the park, and they spent a long day on their shovels and
managed to push it back. Tonight we seem to have it under
control but Howard Sibbald just came over from Banff to
report that there's another big blaze burning down in the
Kananaskis. Tomorrow he and Tex will pull out for there
with most of the police while the rest will stay with me here
to make sure this one doesn't flare up again.

August 28
Today marks the first time I've spent a night in town for
almost three weeks the fires have been so bad. After making
sure that Simpson burn was going nowhere, I was sent over
to Bryant Creek on another mean one, and we only just got
control of it a few days ago.

While in town I dropped into George Noble's photographic
shop, as I promised a couple of the Mounted Police boys a
copy of George's picture of me which won a prize at the
Toronto Fair. I recognized the English lady who waited on
me as the one who I had tipped my hat to a few times on the
street last winter and I struck up a conversation. Her name

is Ethel Wells, George Noble's sister-in-law, and she hails from Sussex. She told me that my picture hangs in the store and many people ask about the wild looking fellow with the piercing eyes. I didn't know what to say to that, so changed the subject by asking her if she would have supper with me some evening next time I'm in town. She's no spring chicken — probably about ten years younger than me — but is very pleasant and seems intent on getting to know the gent attached to the picture she has to look at every day.

XXVII
1921

July 21
Shortly after noon today while patrolling up Sunshine Creek I met Walter Child, a packer for the Wheeler Walking Tour outfit, coming down the trail on the double quick. He informed me that he was on his way to Banff to report the disappearance of Dr. Winthrop Stone and his wife on a climbing expedition to Mount Eon. On questioning him, I found out that they had set off from Wheeler's Assiniboine camp on July 15th to Marvel Pass where Wheeler's head packer, Ralph Rink, had taken their dunnage. There they were to set up a bivouac from which to take on the peak. But they had not returned as expected on the 18th and when some of the other guests failed to find any trace of them by last evening, it was decided to send for help today.

I decided to accompany Child to town to help in any way I could and on arriving reported the news to headquarters and the Mounted Police. Superintendent Stronach was in a tough spot as the area where the Stones had disappeared was outside the park, but he felt that some assistance should be rendered. With his agreement, I volunteered my services to the rescue party to be led by the police, as I know that country better than anyone around here. By late afternoon we had gained permission from the CPR to use one of their best Swiss guides, Rudolph Aemmer, and he along with myself, Child, and Constable Pounder will leave at first light.

July 23
We were off at 5:30 yesterday morning, as it was important that we get to the Mount Assiniboine camp as quickly as possible. It was a hard day's ride, but we arrived late in the afternoon and were informed that a trail gang working in the Wonder Pass area had found the Stone's bivouac camp but no sign of the doctor and his wife. Shortly after our arrival one of the packers, Reno Fitten, returned from a day spent with the trail gang searching the basin between Mount Gloria and Mount Eon — without success. From his description of the territory they had already covered, Rudolph and I agreed that the south side of Eon would probably be the most promising place to examine.

Today we had numerous guests at the camp volunteer to help us, but we felt a small, strong party would be better, so the four of us set out for Wonder Pass. We found the bivouac in the afternoon and spent a good deal of time glassing the slopes for any sign of recent climbing. Nothing was seen and we all agreed that it was highly unlikely, after more than a week that the Stones were still alive. But our job was to find them, alive or not, so tonight around the campfire we planned out a route that would take us to the summit of an outlying spur and give us a good view of the entire south face.

July 24
Its been a day I'll not soon forget — against all possible odds we've been able to rescue Mrs. Stone alive!

As we had planned, we set out early in the morning and fol-lowed the route earlier taken by Fitten around Mount Gloria and into the basin between it and Mount Eon. We then began an relatively easy ascent up to a broad ledge that runs around Eon and out to the summit of the south spur at about the 7,800 foot level, reaching it around noon. Several hours were spent by the whole party glassing the south face in assigned quadrants so that no section would remain unexamined. By late afternoon we had looked at everything at least twice and were just preparing to begin our descent when we all heard a faint cry. It seemed to come from the westward and below us so we all quickly focussed our field glasses on its supposed location. Within a few minutes I was able to pick out the shape of a woman on a thin ledge some quarter of a mile away and about 300 feet downslope. I pointed her out to the others and then drew my Colt and let off a shot to alert her that she had been seen.

We hastily made our way across to her, coming down from above. Once we got immediately over her location it became apparent what had happened. Her rope was tied to a rock on the ledge we were on while the other end dangled ten or twelve feet above her perch on the lower ledge. It was a difficult spot and Rudolph and I, having the most mountain experience, consulted on a plan of rescue. We had lots of rope, so it was decided that I would belay him while he went down to Mrs. Stone. He was by her side in an instant and called up to say that she was very weak and would have to be hauled up. By making a sling with other ropes, he was able to secure her pretty well and with all three of us pulling from above and him pushing from below we carefully lifted her up to our ledge. I immediately looked her over for signs of injury, but other than appearing dazed and weatherbeaten as well as very thin from lack of food there were no outward signs of damage. When Rudolph rejoined us he reported that there was a small trickle of water reaching the ledge, which accounted for her being able to stay alive during her eight day ordeal.

Mrs. Stone was too weak to walk and since Rudolph was the strongest and most experienced on the heights it was left to him to carry her on his back. We made our way carefully along the length of the ledge to a point where we could get off and onto scree slopes and moraines. It was a tremendous feat on his part and quite changed my opinion of at least one Swiss guide. By the time we hit timberline it was getting dark, so I picked out a spot for a bivouac camp and we got Mrs. Stone as warm and comfortable as possible. I've seen what too much food can do to a body that hasn't eaten for many days and warned that we should only make her a little soup for the moment. She is sleeping soundly as I write this, but the rest of us are full of excitement about the days' events and I'm sure we'll be late around the campfire talking about it tonight.

July 26
Yesterday morning Dr. Fred Bell, an Alpine Club member from Winnipeg, arrived at our camp with supplies and took over the care of Mrs. Stone. This allowed us to return to the area where we had discovered her to search for her husband. Before we left to do so, we had to find out for certain if there was any likelihood of him being alive, so Constable Pounder undertook to try interview Mrs. Stone. It was very difficult for her and she broke down several times, which was not surprising when the story came out. Apparently she and Dr. Stone had reached a chimney near the summit of

Mount Eon on July 17th and, finding the rock very rotten, he had told her to take shelter while he went up to investigate the way to the summit. He must have unroped to do so for a few minutes later she heard a noise and a large slab of rock fell past her closely followed by her husband clutching his ice-axe. She braced herself for the rope to go taut, but it didn't and she watched in horror as his body hit a ledge below her and then bounced from one ledge to the next until it was lost to sight. It was in her attempt to descend to the point she had last seen it that she became stranded where we found her.

We've now spent the last two days scouring the slopes below that spot. The weather has been cold and wet, making the climbing very treacherous and the visibility poor. Tomorrow we're going to carry Mrs. Stone in an improvised stretcher over to Marvel Pass as she has now gained enough strength to be moved. We'll have to continue the search for Dr. Stone's body at a later time under better conditions.

July 29
We accomplished the difficult task of carrying Mrs. Stone to Marvel Pass on the 26th and then paused to rest and let her gain more strength for the next leg down to Wheeler's Trail Centre camp. I helped the trail gang clear a good path over to join up with the Wonder Pass trail so that we could keep the distance as short as possible.

Despite our clearing, the carry of the stretcher today was a long and tiring one, covering some fourteen miles. Fortunately, with members of the trail gang assisting, we were able to spell each other off frequently. But the heavy work of the past number of days has taken all the mustard out of us, and tonight a decision was made to leave Mrs. Stone under the care of Dr. Bell at this camp and return to Banff. There a larger party can be organized to continue the search for Dr. Stone's body.

August 2
Returned to Banff yesterday and found that Wheeler had just come into town from his survey work in the north and was organizing a strong party to continue the search, so they won't need me anymore.

The boys have been pestering me with questions and offering their congratulations ever since I got here. Today Howard Sibbald chipped in with his regards as well, saying that it was a fine example of just what this service was set up to do and stating that I had done the whole outfit proud. The accolades are nice, but I just see it as all in a day's work.

* * *

October 14
I came in from the district today to pick up my supplies and there were a couple of nice surprises awaiting me. Harlan Stone, Dr. Stone's brother, wrote from New York to send my share of a sum of money that Mrs. Stone ask be distributed to all those who had participated in her rescue and the recovery of Dr. Stone's body. I sure wasn't expecting to be rewarded for doing my duty, but it is a nice recognition and will certainly come in handy with my upcoming wedding. There was also another compliment in a letter from Walter Wilcox, who is now Secretary of the American Alpine Club.

He informed me that the club will be voting a special resolution of commendation to Rudolph and myself at their meeting in the spring and promised to forward a copy.

Ethel has hiked out to visit me at the Healy Creek cabin on several occasions, and we have been making our plans. We both know that at our ages we're pretty set in our ways, but we agree that we will enjoy each other's company when circumstances allow. As soon as the hunting season is over, I'll continue the work I started last fall on adding to the house and making it fit for a woman's home.

November 15
Ethel and I got hitched today in a quiet little ceremony at the Presbyterian Church, where she is a member of the choir. Walter and Rosabelle and all their brood attended as well as Stephen and Maria from Cochrane, while Ethel was supported by her sister Jessie, her brother Fred, her brother-in-law George Noble and my old friend Will Noble. We went to George's house afterwards to have a bit of a celebration, but since he's a teetotaler it was pretty dry. Ethel and I will now head into Calgary for a few days at the Wales Hotel to enjoy ourselves.

November 21
Good news awaited me when we returned from our little honeymoon in Calgary. I was asked to come down and see Jack Warren, the supervising warden, and was informed that my request to be taken on for permanent service with the wardens has been granted, beginning December 27th. That will put an end to the constant uncertainty about whether I'll be kept on over the winter season, and the guar-

antee of a $100 paycheque each month will put Ethel and me in the pink. I don't think I've had this much luck for twenty years!

Jack said that I'll be on my district all year round now and that I'll have to do a better job of keeping up my diary and reports than I have in the past. We'll see about that, but I guess I better try. I'll have enough writing to keep me busy in any event, so I guess I'll discontinue this journal now. Its always been real interesting to read about what I did and felt in years past and to recall the days when I was young in the mountains. It sure helped to get me through some rough times, but there'll be no more of those now!

Epilogue

The rescue of Mrs. Stone and the achievement of permanent status with the warden service made 1921 the apogee of Bill's career, but certainly not the end of it.

Throughout the twenties and well into the thirties he continued to be the scourge of any lawbreakers in the Healy Creek district, achieving a reputation of being a virtual ghost on the trail. It was said that travellers up Healy Creek would often feel they were being watched while they made camp and that afterwards Bill would suddenly appear and demand "What the Hell are you doing here?" If their answer was satisfactory he would take on a friendlier tone and be helpful and pleasant, but God help those who took offense or were evasive in their reply.

His somewhat elusive behaviour was also reflected in his penchant to forsake the official warden cabins for his own personal abodes that would not be found so easily. His plan to built an alternate shelter on the cliffs behind the Healy Creek cabin was carried out with the construction of a unique two-level cabin built into the rock and accessible only by use of a rope going up its face. At the other end of his district, near the old Bookrest diggings, was the cabin begun in 1914. This he added to over the years with a separate workroom and an elaborate set of doors that could be barred to keep out unwanted guests. Apart from these there were other smaller shelters he built hidden deep in the bush off the beaten track, some which undoubtedly have not been found to this day. However, he often did leave a sign of ownership on the window or door of his cabins, an owl sitting on a branch. He also carved owls and made them out of pieces of log burl, and given the owl's shyness and stealth they were undoubtedly meant to be self portraits.

Another famous sign of Bill's adorned the official Healy Creek cabin. Set in his ways, he did not see eye to eye with the equally tough superintendent of Rocky Mountains Park, P. J. Jennings, who ruled the park with an iron hand in the early thirties. Since the superintendent would frequently go on inspection tours, Bill attached a sign to the cabin for his benefit that read "Pass me by O gentle Jennings."

By the late twenties changes were afoot in the warden service with respect to predators that Bill was deathly opposed to. For many years wardens had been allowed to keep the skins of any predators they killed in the course of their duties, excepting bears, with the idea that it would help to supplement their income. Most were coyotes and although Bill sometimes did not bother himself, he supported the policy and was opposed to changes in it introduced by J. B. Harkin in the late twenties because of the effect it would have on men with families, like his brother Walter. He and Walter also seem to have been the most accomplished wardens at eliminating coyotes, as Harkin noted in a letter in 1935 that out of thirty-five coyotes taken in the park that fiscal year "twenty were taken by the Peytos."

In December, 1927 Bill decided to challenge the new rules about the keeping of pelts after he had killed an exceptionally fine specimen of mountain lion near the Healy Creek cabin in November. When Jack Warren read his diary entry, he asked what Bill had done with the animal's hide and was told it had been sent off to make a mat as it was "his property." Eventually Harkin found out about the matter and asked the superintendent what action had been taken with respect to the hide and demanded a report justifying the killing. Bill was in no hurry to respond, but when he did over a month later he explained that the lion had killed three deer within fifty feet of his cabin and had lain in sight of its most recent kill all day. This, he said, was unusual and indicated that the lion presented a danger to humans. In this case he won the battle, as his explanation was accepted, but lost the war, as he eventually agreed to turn the hide over "when next he was in town."

Bill's disagreements with the government were not limited to those arising from his employment. He remained bitter about his inability to reap any reward from his work at the Bookrest, and this would be exacerbated by his experiences trying to develop his talc claims. Initially he did little work on them, contenting himself with taking out enough material to do carvings for his own pleasure that were given to friends or nieces and nephews. Eventually the Black Diamond claim, which had been staked for his brother Walter, lapsed for lack of development work, but in 1927 Bill restaked it as the Gold Dollar in his wife Ethel's name. As it turned out, the mining recorder had done so incorrectly since the right to stake a claim in what had become Kootenay National Park in 1919 had lapsed with the signing of the Banff-Windermere Highway agreement between Canada and British Columbia.

Finally all Bill's years of prospecting and mining seemed to be leading to some real success when he signed an option agreement on February 9, 1927 with the National Talc Company, headed by Sir Henry Pellatt of Toronto. National Talc secured permission from the Department of the Interior to construct a wagon road from Massive Siding up Redearth and Pharaoh Creeks and over Redearth Pass to the claims. But the Department refused to recognize the Gold Dollar claim as valid because of the mistake in registering it. This made Bill furious, and thereafter he had "no use for the government." Bill Aubin of Banff recalled that Bill would sometimes come into his blacksmith shop carrying his rifle and would start talking about the talc mine and the government. He would get so riled up he would bang the floor with the butt of the gun to the point that Aubin would take cover for fear of it going off.

By 1930 National Talc had spent $18,000 on building a bridge over the Bow, putting in a tote road and constructing two cabins at the mine. But this was not enough for Bill as little actual development work on the Red Mountain claim had been carried out and he had received no money. He therefore cancelled National Talc's option to purchase and entered into a new agreement with Western Talc Holdings of Calgary. They sunk five drillholes in 1931 but perhaps due to poor results or the lack of financing in the Depression they ceased operations. The claim was kept in good standing until 1938, but it appears that Bill never received a cent from it.

In his personal life, Bill became even more eccentric as his length of service spent alone in the district increased. He and his wife Ethel seem to have spent very little time together, although this certainly was not uncommon for wardens during the period as they were only allowed one day a month in town to resupply. She apparently did spend part of each summer at the Healy Creek cabin and the rest of the year would come out for visits to bring him food, often accompanied by members of her family. Her sister-in-law, Helen Wells, recalled that when they went out to Healy Creek Bill would come and meet them at the ford of the Bow and remind them that he didn't want any talking as one had to always be quiet in the woods and that while visiting they had to haul their own water and chop their own wood. On these trips Ethel often left behind some pickled chicken or other meat but Bill usually wouldn't touch it and told another visitor that he thought his wife was trying to poison him.

Bill's relationship with his son Robert also never seems to have developed to the extent that he had hoped, probably for similar reasons of lack of opportunity. Robert Peyto completed his schooling in Armstrong, B.C. and after graduation went to Vancouver to find work. He first joined the army and later the navy, in which he served during the Second World War, and like his father was wounded in the leg. Eventually he went to work at a dockyard in Esquimalt and in 1966 retired to Shawnigan Lake, B.C. After Bill's retirement in 1936, he seems to have gone to the coast a few times to visit his son and Robert also came to Banff occasionally.

Bill did keep on good terms with his other relatives, who by the 1930s were numerous in Banff. His brother and co-worker Walter and his wife Rosabelle lived across Banff Avenue from him with their large family of six children. Bill was kind to the children and would often tell them stories or carve some special thing for them as a present. Similarly, his brother Stephen and his family, who had gone into the dairy business in Cochrane, moved to Anthracite in 1923 to start a dairy and market garden, and he spent time with them as well.

By 1930 Bill had begun to slow down due to his age and the hard life he had lived. He was particularly bothered by arthritis in his hands, and his old war wounds. These had resulted in his confinement to the Belcher Hospital for war veterans in Calgary for a two week period in October, 1929. This situation was aggravated on August 2, 1930 when he was bucked off his horse while patrolling fourteen miles west of Banff. He got back on and rode into town, but when examined by Dr. G. M. Atkin he found that he had injured himself in the groin and had aggravated his war wound in the right thigh. He was granted medical leave until August 11th, at which point he immediately saddled up and headed back out to his district. But the pain was so excruciating he was back to see Atkin within a week and was granted a further medical leave. When he came back on duty, Jack Warren offered to find him work around Banff, but Bill made it clear that he preferred to be out of town and he returned to the Healy Creek district in December.

During the '30s the warden service began to change considerably as a new generation of men came on staff and the importance of training increased. Annual training schools informed wardens on the latest fire fighting techniques and equipment, game and fish management practises, technological advances and so on. Bill begrudgingly took part in these schools but preferred the ways he was more familiar with. Several pieces of evidence exist that showed he remained firmly of the "old school."

Park wardens were expected to work seven days a week and to work sufficient hours to get the job done, which would usually mean about ten hours a day or unlimited hours in the case of an emergency. Personnel records were kept for each employee and Bill noted in his official record in October, 1933 under the category of Days of Month "Every day" and Hours per day "Average 19." To the question of whether he worked regular hours he answered "No" and under the section asking for details he stated "In his district a warden is on duty all the time." Similarly, when in 1934 it was decided to pair wardens up over the winter months due to the isolation of the occupation, Bill was the only district warden to be left on his own.

In the 1930s the dispute between parks administration and the wardens in the field became even more intense when quotas were set for killing of predators at the same time as the use of traps for the purpose was banned. During the period there was a strongly held belief that cougars were killing a great deal of park game and that the "shooting only" policy meant that few would be eradicated because of their stealth and nocturnal habits. Bill regarded cougars as the smartest of the parks' animals and had a healthy respect for them. Wardens were allowed to keep dogs at this time to assist with predator control and Bill had two, named Rags and Danger. Pat Brewster recalled coming upon Bill on the Healy Creek trail on one occasion and noticing that his dog looked like "an elongated tortoise." Bill informed him that the dog had been attacked by a cougar and he had made him a coat of rawhide to protect him if it should occur again.

In September, 1932 the Crag and Canyon *reported that Bill had killed a "big lion" near Healy Creek. According to the story he was riding along the trail when his horse detected the cougar and Bill sent Danger to give chase. The dog treed the cat in a short distance and Bill came up and killed him with his rifle. When he skinned the animal out the pelt measured eight feet. The newspaper noted that it was not often that wardens got an opportunity to destroy mountain lions and called for a change in policy that would allow organized hunts for them. Not everyone supported a campaign against cougars as ideas about conservation and predator control were just beginning to change at the time. A few years later, in 1935, Banff naturalist Dan McCowan wrote an article in the newspaper complaining about a new park initiative against cougars, and this elicited a letter of response from Bill, the only time he was known to speak out publicly on any issue and indicating quite firmly where he stood on this one:*

"After reading the article of Mr. Dan McCowan on the

animal life of the Park, I became interested, as I have studied animal life in all its phases for quite a number of years. I
have collected fossils of several periods; the skulls of most
all of our animal life and have studied the animals in life in
all seasons and occasionally have kept some animals alive in
order to study. Have done likewise with our birds. I have
also collected specimens from ancient Indian camps; have
collected the minerals in the mountains and have studied
the rock formations etc. The genial Dan must have been suffering under a greater strain than he realized, due to his
arduous lecture tour, or he would not have given out any
such interview.

I'm quite sure that he would not be looking for such a low
controversy as is sometimes indulged in by some natural-
ists, and the people of Banff should persuade him to take a
long holiday during the coming summer."

*In November, 1933 the government passed an Order-in-Council
stipulating that anyone who became sixty-five years of age after
December 31, 1933 be retired from active duty unless exempted
before attaining that age. As there were records in department files
that indicated Bill had given his birthdate variously as February
14, 1875 and February 14, 1876 and yet had indicated on a medical form in 1930 that he was sixty-three, this matter was of some
importance. Bill swore a declaration that his true date of birth was
February 14, 1869 and that forestalled the issue for a couple of
months. Superintendent Jennings interviewed him in January,
1934 and Bill indicated that because of the state of his health he
would not be able to carry on much longer, but that he would make
himself available for special assignments as needed. Arrangements
for his retirement were being made when members of the warden
service obviously decided that they couldn't do without him and he*

was granted the necessary exemption on the understanding that we would do "special work" controlling mountain lions and other predators and preventing the depredations of beavers.

Bill was exempted one further year in February, 1935 in order to continue his "special work," but in April of that year he had to spend another two weeks in the Belcher recovering from pain in his old wound in the right thigh and weakness in his knee joints. In November Jennings reported that "he has not exhibited any great zeal in hunting mountain lions, which is possibly due to his advancing years and his war disability" and therefore was not prepared to request a further exemption. Bill did not argue the point and was granted a three month's retiring leave with pay from the date of his official retirement on February 14, 1936 in recognition of his long service.

The pension for his years with the government combined with his small war disability pension was enough to keep he and Ethel going. But after a life spent on the move in the wilds, boredom with town life quickly set in. By May, 1936 Bill was writing Harkin to request that he be appointed "honourary warden" from the date of the completion of his retirement leave. Harkin looked into the matter and found that an honourary warden had all the powers of a regular warden but received no pay for his services. It is not known whether Bill ever served in this capacity, but if he did it was shortlived for he soon had his hands full when Ethel became ill. Much of his time for the next few years was spent caring for her until her death in July, 1940 at the age of sixty-two.

Alone again, Bill's last years were spent out in the wilderness he loved, as much as his health would allow. He concentrated on his now extensive collections of fossils and minerals, once more col-

laborating with Norman Sanson, who had also retired. He likely built a few more hidden cabins so that he could get away from civilization, but they were now closer to town because of his lack of mobility. Having served in two wars, he still felt he had something to offer his country in a third, but was turned down when he tried to enlist in Calgary.

Early in the spring of 1943, Jim Simpson ran into Bill and he told him he "had a misery in his insides and his plumbing was out of order." By the middle of March the doctor had ordered him into the Belcher for treatment and it was discovered he had cancer. He died there on Friday, March 24th just having past his seventy-fourth birthday. He was laid to rest on March 28th in a simple military grave next to his beloved Emily in the Banff Cemetery.

Tributes to Bill's memory were spoken and recorded in many places in the years after his death. Jim Simpson called him "the most original character I have ever met," and Pat Brewster spoke of him as "one of the great personalities of the mountains." But perhaps he was best summed up in the very personal obituary which appeared in the Crag and Canyon *after his death:*

"With the passing of "Bill" Peyto one of the oldest and most colourful links with the early days of Banff Park, and indeed Western Canada, has been broken. . . . "Bill's" knowledge of the Rocky Mountains area was equalled by few and surpassed by none. Indefatigable when on the trail he gave everything to ensure the success of his party. His knowledge of the wild animals of the district, their habits and peculiarities, was tremendous and fortunate indeed was the hunter who secured his services as guide. Utterly fearless and at all times willing to assume any risk to safeguard those in his charge he was one of the most popular and best beloved of the "riders of the trails." . . .

To say that a very gallant gentleman passed from among us is but to give utterance to a trite statement, but those who really knew "Bill" will realize that something has gone out of their lives that nothing can replace. A faithful friend, a patriotic, though unassuming citizen and a gentleman in the highest sense of the word, the town is greatly the poorer by his passing, for we shall not look upon his like again.

Peace to his ashes and "Good Hunting."

Amen.

Wilcox's shot of me on Chiniquay in 1895

Ralph Edwards (mounted) and myself (seated) being entertained by
Dave White and his sister Lizzie on their violins, 1895

Myself (right) and our party visiting Joe Smith (second left), 1897

A day off in camp with Collie and Baker, 1897

The boys and myself (right) at Field after coming down the Blaeberry, 1897

Getting ready to leave with a party from my place on the Bow about 1902

The take of marten pelts from the Saskatchewan country, 1899

Reading a geology paper at our home on the Bow about 1903

Emily and myself ready to start to Cascade with the Longstaff family, Aug. 1903

Myself (left) and brother-in-law Jim Wood (standing) with the German party on the Athabasca, 1904

Emily in the beautiful country near the Bookrest, 1903

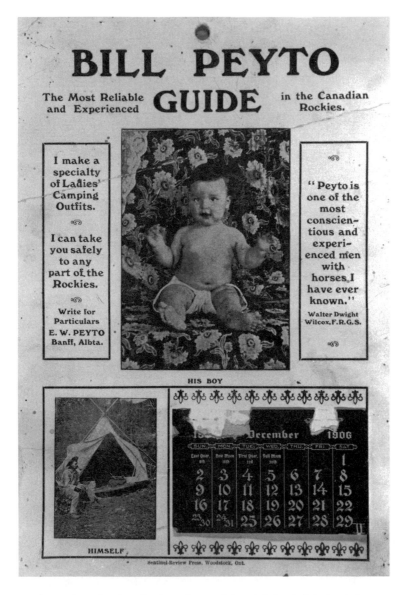

This is the calendar I had made to celebrate Robin's first birthday

Bringing in the lynx to the zoo after some fun at the Alberta bar, 1909

On patrol near Simpson Summit about 1921

Mr. Knechtel's picture of Lightning and me at the Bookrest, 1913

George Noble's photograph of me that won a prize at the Toronto Fair and caught me a wife

Acknowledgements

I would like to thank the staff at the Whyte Museum of the Canadian Rockies for their assistance in finding material for this story. All photographs are from the Archives of the Whyte Museum. Particular thanks go to Craig Richards and Jim Swanson of the Technical Services department for their assistance with photography and design.

I would also like to thank the staff at the Federal Records Centre in Edmonton for their assistance with Bill Peyto's personnel records and other warden records in their repository.

Finally, and most importantly, I would like to acknowlege the assistance of Banff poet and writer Gordon Burles with this work. Gordon began to investigate Bill Peyto's background and life some twenty-five years ago and without the information he found and recorded at that time and since then, this book could not have been completed in its current form. Gordon also read the manuscript and offered very helpful advice on some of the incidents mentioned and on the use of language consistent with Bill's vocabulary.